Interest-Rate Swaps

INTEREST-RATE SWAPS

Brian Coyle

Apart from any fair dealing for the purpose of research or private study, or criticism or review, as permitted under the Copyright, Designs and Patents Act 1988, this publication may be reproduced, stored or transmitted, in any form or by any means, only with the prior permission in writing of the publisher, or in the case of reprographic reproduction in accordance with the terms and licences issued by the Copyright Licensing Agency. Enquiries concerning reproduction outside those terms should be addressed to the publisher's agents at the undermentioned address:

Financial World Publishing
IFS House
4-9 Burgate Lane
Canterbury
Kent
CT1 2XJ
United Kingdom

Telephone: 01227 818687

Financial World Publishing publications are published by
The Chartered Institute of Bankers, a non-profit-making registered educational charity.

The Chartered Institute of Bankers believes that the sources of information upon which this book is based are reliable and has made every effort to ensure the complete accuracy of the text. However, neither CIB, the author nor any contributor can accept any legal responsibility whatsoever for consequences that may arise from errors or omissions or any opinion or advice given.

Typeset by Kevin O'Connor
Printed in Italy

© The Chartered Institute of Bankers 2001

ISBN 0-85297-443-4

Contents

1	Introduction	1
2	What are Interest-Rate Swaps?	5
3	Uses of Liability Swaps	21
4	The Role of Banks	43
5	Swaps Rates	53
6	Matched Swap Payments	65
7	Asset Swaps	73
8	Non-Generic Swaps	83
9	Valuation of Swaps	91
10	Administration of Swaps	103
11	Swaps and Financial Risk	115
	Appendix: Zero Coupon Rates	125
	Glossary	137
	Index	145

Introduction

Swaps have become an important instrument in the management of the assets and liabilities of a business. As its name implies, a swap is a contract between two parties who agree to exchange a stream of payments over an agreed period, typically several years.

Types of Swap

There are several types of swap:

- interest-rate swaps
- currency swaps
- equity swaps (or equity-linked swaps)
- commodity swaps.

In an interest-rate swap, the parties exchange interest payments on a notional amount of principal. Typically, one party pays a fixed rate of interest on the principal for the term of the swap, and the other party pays a floating rate of interest that is periodically adjusted.

A currency swap also involves an exchange of interest payments, but with one party paying interest on a notional amount of principal in one currency, and the other party paying interest on a notional principal amount in a different currency. The currency risk is eliminated by an exchange of principal amounts at the end of the term of the swap.

In an equity swap, the two parties exchange a stream of payments based on the performance of an underlying quantity of equity shares or an equity share index.

A commodity swap is an agreement during which the parties exchange cash flows based on the price of a commodity such as jet fuel oil, other grades of fuel oil, and natural gas. One party pays a fixed price on an underlying quantity of the commodity and the other pays a floating price, usually based on the average price of the commodity over a period of time.

A distinction is also made for conventional currency and interest rate swaps between

- liability swaps and
- asset swaps.

A liability swap enables a borrower to modify his/her liabilities, for example to swap a fixed-rate liability on debts for a floating-rate liability, or a debt in one currency for a liability in another. Liability swaps therefore are an instrument for the management of debts or liabilities.

An asset swap is used to alter the nature of the income stream from an investment (asset), typically by exchanging a fixed rate of income for a floating-rate income stream, or vice versa. An asset swap therefore is an instrument for asset management.

The structure of asset swaps and liability swaps are the same. The terms are used to distinguish the purpose of the swap, not its structure.

The purpose of this book is to describe what interest rate swaps are, why they are used, who uses them, when and how.

What are Interest-Rate Swaps?

An interest-rate swap is an agreement between two parties to exchange one stream of interest payments for another stream with different features. Interest payments are calculated on an agreed amount of notional principal and for an agreed period of time. They are exchanged at regular intervals on either a fixed or a floating-rate basis.

- Fixed-rate payments are at an interest rate agreed at the outset and applied throughout the term of the swap.
- Floating-rate payments are at a rate of interest that is periodically reset, with reference to an agreed benchmark rate of interest, such as the London Interbank Offered Rate (LIBOR). For swaps with six-monthly exchanges of payments, floating-rate payments commonly are set at the six-month LIBOR rate or possibly at a spread above or below six-month LIBOR. The amount of each swap payment varies with the change in LIBOR since the previous payment.

Coupon Swaps

The most common type of interest-rate swap involves the exchange of a stream of variable-rate payments against a stream of fixed-rate payments, for example 6% per annum fixed against six-month LIBOR. This type of swap is called either

- a fixed/floating rate swap, or
- a coupon swap.

Coupon Swap: Swap Payments

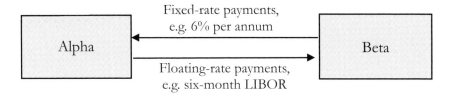

In the coupon swap illustrated above, Alpha agrees to make payments to Beta at a floating rate of interest, in this example is six-month LIBOR on the notional principal. In return, Beta agrees to make payments at a fixed rate of interest, in this example is 6% per annum. The exchange of payments is likely to be every six months.

The fixed payments are known amounts. The floating payments are not known when the swap is transacted, and depend on movements over time in the floating-rate index or benchmark rate that is used.

In a simple swap arrangement, the timing of the payments by each party to the other will coincide. However, swaps commonly are negotiated in which the payments do not coincide.

Basis Swaps

Basis swaps are less common than coupon swaps. They involve the exchange of a stream of variable-rate payments for another variable-rate stream but on a different interest-rate basis; for example three-month LIBOR against six-month LIBOR, or six-month LIBOR against a six-month Certificate of Deposit rate. Basis swaps also are called floating/floating swaps.

Basis Swaps: Swap Payments

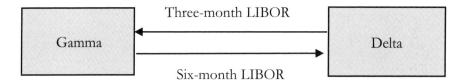

Generic Swap (Plain Vanilla Swap)

A generic swap, also called a plain vanilla swap, is a swap with standard terms and no modifications. The features of a generic swap are:

- a constant amount of notional principal over the full term or tenor of the swap
- an exchange of fixed-interest payments against floating-rate payments (a coupon swap)
- a fixed rate that is constant throughout the term or tenor of the swap
- the floating-rate payments calculated on a flat floating-rate index with no margin above or below the index. For example, interest payable at six-month LIBOR, not at 25 basis points (0.25%) above six-month LIBOR or 100 basis points (1%) below six-month LIBOR
- regular payments of fixed and floating-rate interest by one party to the other, although payment dates need not coincide
- no special features
- an immediate (spot) start date.

Banks as Intermediaries

Many banks use swaps to hedge their own interest-rate exposures. A number of banks also specialize as intermediaries in the swaps market, and

- arrange swaps between two other parties, or

- act as principal, i.e. as one of the parties in a swap with a customer.

Example

A swaps bank identifies two customers with matching but opposite swap requirements.

- Alpha wishes to pay floating-rate interest on $30 million and receive a fixed rate
- Beta wishes to receive floating-rate interest on a similar amount, and to pay a fixed rate.

Instead of arranging a swap directly between Alpha and Beta, the bank could arrange two matching swaps, in each of which it is one of the parties.

- In Swap 1 with Alpha, the bank might arrange to pay a fixed rate, for example 5.70%, and receive dollar LIBOR.
- In Swap 2, with Beta, the bank may arrange to receive a fixed rate, of 5.74%, for example and pay dollar LIBOR.

Swaps Bank as Intermediary

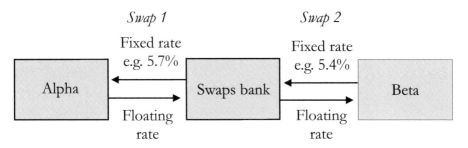

The bank will make a turn, or profit, from the difference between the fixed rate received and the fixed rate paid, taking the two swap agreements together. In this example, the turn is 0.04% (5.74% receivable minus 5.70% payable) or four basis points, yielding a net income of $12,000 per annum on notional principal of $30 million.

In practise, it is difficult to identify customers with swap requirements that match exactly. Specialist banks therefore establish a swaps book, i.e. they agree to act as a counterparty in a swap without looking for another customer with a matching but opposite requirement. The role of banks in the swaps market is described in more detail in Chapter 4.

Notional Principal

Swap payments are calculated by applying the agreed rate of interest to an agreed amount of notional principal. For the floating-rate payment, the rate payable on the notional principal for an interest period is set at the start of the period, and the payment is made at the end of the period.

For example, suppose that Alpha and Beta have arranged a swap on a notional principal of $10 million, in which Alpha pays a fixed rate of 7% per annum and receives payments from Beta at 12-month LIBOR, with swap payments exchanged once a year. Suppose that the 12-month LIBOR rate at the end of Year 1 is 8% per annum. The floating rate applicable to Year 2 and payable at the end of Year 2 will be 8%. Swap payments at the end of Year 2 therefore would be:

Alpha to Beta (fixed)	$700,000
Beta to Alpha (floating)	$800,000

In practise, there simply would be a net payment of $100,000 by Beta to Alpha.

The notional principal can be in any major currency, although the most active market is in dollars. Other frequently used currencies are yen, euros and sterling.

The minimum amount of notional principal against which banks are prepared to transact swaps is $5 million or £5 million, but swaps can be arranged for much larger amounts, of $200 million or more. Banks sometimes agree to smaller deals for customers with whom they have good relationships.

Interest for each period is calculated using the appropriate interest rate convention. This might be an Actual/360-day basis, an Actual/365-day basis, a 30/360-day basis or an Actual/Actual basis, depending on whether the rate payable is fixed or floating, and on interest-rate conventions that apply to the particular currency. In the examples in this book, interest payments are shown as an approximate amount only, for the sake of clarity. For example, interest payable in a six-month period will be calculated as 6/12 of the annual rate, and applied to the notional principal.

Swap Payments

Swap payments are based on notional principal; there is no actual exchange of principal and no loan between the two parties to a swap. It is convenient to refer to the exchange of interest payments on the swap, but technically this is incorrect because there is no loan. Swap payments are described more accurately as an exchange of payments, calculated as a percentage rate of a notional principal sum.

The swap agreement specifies the regularity of payments. Exchange of payments commonly is every six months, but might be every three months, every year etc., to suit the requirements of the parties to the agreement.

Each party to a swap undertakes to make a payment to the other at regular intervals, but in practise when the payment dates coincide usually there is only a single net payment from one to the other each time. The net payment is made by the party that owes the greater amount. The payments between the parties need not coincide. One party to a swap might undertake to make a series of interest payments on one set of dates, and the other party might make its payments on a different set of dates.

Example
Blue and Purple arrange a swap with the following terms:

Tenor: Three years
Notional principal: $10 million

Blue: Pays fixed rate of 7.5% per annum.
Annual payments.

Purple: Pays floating rate of six-month dollar LIBOR.
Six-monthly payments.

Analysis
Suppose that six-month LIBOR for each payment date is as follows:

		Payment based on six-month dollar LIBOR
		%
Year 1	Month 6	6.8
	Month 12	7.2
Year 2	Month 6	8.0
	Month 12	8.4
Year 3	Month 6	7.7
	Month 12	7.2

Payments under the swap agreement would be as shown in the diagram opposite.

Payments Under Swap Agreement

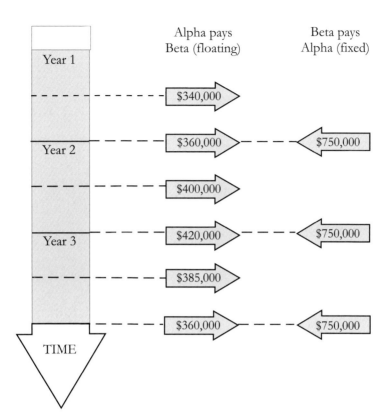

Note:
The floating-rate payments are approximate amounts only. Actual interest payments would be calculated, for dollars, on an Actual/360-day interest-rate basis.

Netting of Payments
When both parties are due to make a payment on the same date, there could be a simple net payment from one party to the other. However, this will depend on the terms of the swap agreement. An agreement could provide for two gross payments of interest rather than a single net payment from one party to the other.

Example
Yellow and Red arrange a swap with the following terms:

Tenor:	Four years
Notional principal:	£10 million
Yellow:	Pays fixed rate of 6% per annum. Six-monthly payments.
Purple:	Pays floating rate of six-month sterling LIBOR. Six-monthly payments, on the same dates as payments by Yellow.

Analysis
Suppose that when the first payments fall due after six months, the applicable six-month LIBOR rate is 5%.

Yellow will pay Red	£300,000 (6/12 x 6% x £10 million)
Red will pay Yellow	£250,000 (6/12 x 5% x £10 million)

Note
These interest payments are approximate amounts, actual interest payments would be calculated on the appropriate interest rate convention that in the case of sterling will be an Actual/365-day basis for the floating-rate interest.

If the swap agreement provides for the netting of payments, Yellow simply would pay Red the difference between the amounts due, i.e. £500,000. If the swap agreement provides for gross payments, Yellow must pay £300,000 in full and Red must pay £250,000.

Exercise
A company arranges a swap with its bank, in which the company is a payer of 7.60% fixed and a receiver of six-month LIBOR. The notional principal is £40 million and the parties to the transaction agree to six-monthly settlement of payments by means of a net payment on each settlement date.

On a reset date on 5 September, six-month LIBOR is 8.40%. What payment is due and when will it be paid?

Solution

	%
Company pays	7.60
Company receives	8.40
Company receives net	0.80

For the six-month interest-rate period, the amount receivable from the swap bank is £160,000 (£40 million x 6/12 x 0.80%). Typically, the payment will be due on the 4 March, at the end of the six-month period. By setting the variable-interest rate in September, at the start of the interest period, each party to the swap knows well in advance what the net payment or receipt will be on the next payment date.

Receiver and Payer

Both parties receive interest and pay interest in a swap. It is usual, however, to identify the two parties in a coupon swap as

- the fixed rate receiver, and
- the fixed rate payer.

Rates Received and Paid: Swap Rates

The rates in a swap, i.e. the fixed-rate received/paid, is subject to negotiation between the swaps bank and the customer. Rates are described more fully in Chapter 5, but briefly

- in a generic (plain-vanilla) swap, the floating rate is a flat rate, but non-generic swaps can be arranged in which the floating rate payment is a benchmark index rate plus or minus an agreed number of basis points, e.g. six-month LIBOR plus 30 basis points.
- The fixed rate is related to the yield obtainable on government

securities, e.g. US Treasuries for swaps in dollars, and gilts for swaps in sterling, etc., for government bonds with the same maturity as the swap. The swap fixed rate usually is higher than the comparable government bond rate that is a risk-free rate of interest. Historically, however, the size of the spread over government bond rates has varied. For dollar swaps, fixed rates might be quoted and traded at an explicit spread above Treasuries, e.g. the Treasury bond rate plus 40 basis points, whereas in most other currencies it is usual to quote and trade swaps at an absolute fixed rate.

Dates

When a swap is made, there are several dates to consider.

- The transaction date or trade date is the date when the parties agree to enter into the swap.
- The effective date for a swap is the date from which the fixed and floating-rate payments begin to accrue.
- A reset date or fixing date is the date when the floating swap rate is reset.
- The maturity date is the end of the term of the swap.

For example, two parties might agree on June 5 to enter into a three-year coupon swap, starting from June 12 Year 1, and ending on June 12 Year 4, in which swap payments are exchanged every six months. The transaction date in this example is June 5 Year 1, the effective date is June 12 Year 1, reset dates are every six months and maturity date is June 12 Year 4.

This is shown in the diagram opposite.

Dates

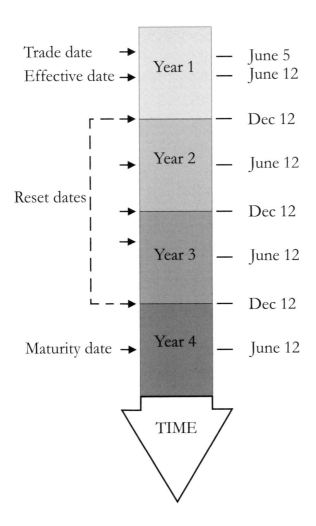

Term of a Swap

Swap agreements can be for a term of up to ten years or sometimes longer. Typical maturities are two, three, four, five, seven or ten years, although swaps also are used by banks (interbank swaps) for short-term interest-rate exposure management of one year or less. A large (non-bank) company might use swaps over a two-to-ten-year period.

Medium-term swaps are now available in most freely traded (convertible) currencies. In the most liquid of currencies, swaps sometimes are available with maturities in excess of 20 years for the best credits, i.e. governments of advanced economies. Swaps in excess of ten years are fairly uncommon, but are becoming less so. They might be arranged only if a swaps bank can match two parties with opposite requirements at the same time.

Summary

Features of Swaps

Size of swaps	The notional principal varies from one swap arrangement to another, but is usually not less than $5 million, £5 million or €5 million. Banks might arrange much smaller swaps for clients.
Term/maturity/tenor	Normally ten years or less; typically three to five years. However, interbank money-market swaps of three to six-months are common, arranged as part of the short-term interest-rate management of each bank. Many swaps have a standard tenor of one, two, three, four, five, seven or ten years, but many variations are possible.
Role of banks	A bank might arrange a swap on its own behalf to manage its interest-rate position, and many swaps are interbank swaps. Some banks specialise in swaps, dealing for profit.
Currencies	The dollar is the major currency in the swaps market. Other currencies include euros, yen, sterling, Australian dollars, Canadian dollars and Swiss francs.
Over-the-counter	Swaps are over-the-counter (OTC) instruments and not exchange-traded, although there are

some swap futures. They have the characteristics of OTC products:
- Bilateral – just two parties to any swap.
- Customized – to suit the requirements of a specific customer.
- Not usually margined, unlike traded options and futures, for example, where payment of a deposit, a margin or performance bond is required to protect the exchange against credit risk.
- Can be cancelled with the original counterparty only, although swaps can be traded on a secondary market.
- Prices are negotiable/negotiated.

Uses of Liability Swaps

Most liability swaps are coupon swaps. The successful development of interest-rate liability swaps since the early 1980s can be attributed to their various uses that include:

- altering the mix of fixed-rate and floating-rate debt in a company's funding structure, perhaps to hedge interest rate exposures in anticipation of a rise or a fall in interest rates
- obtaining fixed-interest-rate funds when only variable-rate borrowing is available in the primary loan and bond markets
- obtaining a lower rate of interest on borrowings as a consequence of the swap (credit arbitrage). Because of credit arbitrage, both parties to a swap can benefit from lower borrowing costs.

Changing the Basis of Interest Payments

A coupon swap (fixed/floating swap) was derived from the perception that there are companies borrowing at a fixed rate of interest that would prefer to borrow at a variable rate, and companies borrowing at a variable rate that would prefer to borrow at a fixed rate.

A company might have a loan on which it pays variable-rate interest, but would prefer the loan to be at a fixed rate of interest. It could repay the variable-rate loan and take out a replacement fixed-rate loan, but would incur termination costs and arrangement fees. Alternatively, it could use a coupon swap to change the basis of its payments from floating to fixed rate.

Similarly, a company with a fixed-rate loan might wish to pay its interest at a variable rate. It could redeem the loan and borrow at a variable rate. Alternatively, it could keep the fixed-rate loan but arrange a swap to change into a variable-rate payment profile.

Example 1
A UK company borrowing at six-month LIBOR plus 100 basis points (1%) wishes to swap its variable-rate interest liability for a fixed-rate liability. A bank is willing to arrange a swap where it would receive fixed payments at 6.5% per annum against payment of six-month LIBOR, with six-monthly exchanges.

Analysis
The company is paying interest at LIBOR plus 1%. The effect of the swap will be as follows.

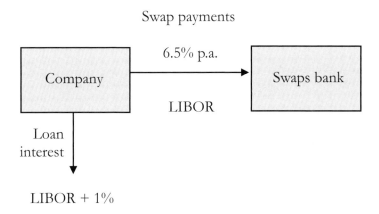

The interest payments on the variable loan are at LIBOR plus 1%, and receipts under the swap arrangement are at LIBOR. The LIBOR-related payment and LIBOR-related receipt cancel each other out, leaving the company a net payer at a fixed rate of interest.

The net result is that the company will alter its payments profile from a variable rate at LIBOR plus 1% to a fixed rate of 7.5%. This is illustrated over the page.

		%
Loan interest:	Pay	- (LIBOR + 1%)
Swap:	Receive	LIBOR
	Pay	- 6.5
Net payment		- 7.5

As a result of this swap arrangement, the company has not changed its loan. It still has a variable-rate loan for which it is contractually liable to the lender, and on which it pays interest at a variable rate. The swap, however, allows the company to switch from variable-rate payments to net fixed-rate payments, taking the loan and the swap payments together.

Example 2
A company has issued $50 million of eurobonds at a fixed rate of 8% per annum. The bonds have five years remaining to redemption. The company would like to pay interest at a variable rate, and a bank would be willing to arrange a five-year swap on notional principal of $50 million in which the company pays a floating rate at LIBOR and receives a fixed rate of 7.5% per annum. The effect of the swap would be:

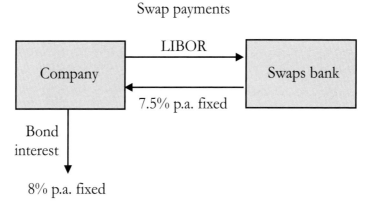

The fixed-interest payments on the bond are partly canceled out by the fixed-rate receipts under the swap. The net result is that the company will alter the basis of its payments from a fixed rate to a net floating rate of LIBOR plus 50 basis points (0.50%) per annum.

USES OF LIABILITY SWAPS

		%
Bond coupon:	Pay	- 8.00
Swap:	Receive	+ 7.50
	Pay	- LIBOR
Net payment		- (LIBOR + 0.50)

The company has not changed its debt obligations, and is still liable for the bonds and the 8% interest coupon payments. The swap, however, creates a switch from fixed-rate to net floating-rate payments, taking the bond interest and the swap payments together.

Exercise

Attempt your own solution to the following problem.

A large corporation has a floating-rate loan at six-month LIBOR plus 75 basis points, with five years remaining to maturity. A European investment bank issues a five-year dollar bond at 7%, paying interest every six months.

The corporation and the bank want to arrange a coupon swap. The corporation wants to pay a fixed rate, and the bank wants to receive a fixed rate of 7.3%.

What might be the terms of a suitable interest-rate coupon swap between the corporation and the bank? What would be the net interest cost for the corporation as a result, assuming that the bank is a receiver of fixed interest at 7.30%?

Solution

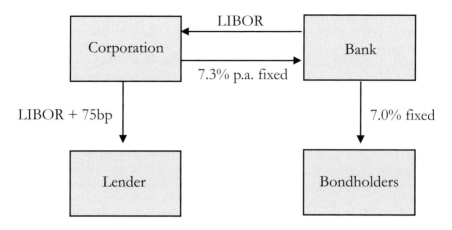

A suitable swap might be a five-year swap with six-monthly payments, in which the bank is a receiver of fixed interest at 7.30% against six-month dollar LIBOR. The notional principal would be negotiable, but probably an amount roughly equal to the corporation's floating-rate liabilities.

As a result of the swap, the corporation would switch from being a payer of interest at a floating rate to a net payer at a fixed rate, taking its loan and the swap payments together.

		%
Loan interest:	Pay	- (LIBOR + 0.75%)
Swap:	Receive	LIBOR
	Pay	- 7.30 fixed
Net payment		- 8.05 fixed

Why Change the Basis of Interest Payments?

A coupon swap is a long-term agreement binding a company to either pay or receive a specific fixed rate of interest in exchange for a variable rate. A company using a coupon swap to alter the basis of its interest-rate payments might have a strong view about either future interest-rate movements over the term of the swap, or the most suitable mix of fixed-rate and variable-rate debt in its funding structure, or the most suitable mix of fixed and variable-rate items in its debt or loan investment portfolio.

There are four main reasons for wanting to swap from floating to fixed-rate payments or vice versa:

- to change the mix between fixed-rate and floating-rate debt in the company's funding structure
- inability to borrow in the financial markets at a fixed rate
- to anticipate an increase or fall in interest rates, and to switch to fixed-rate or variable-rate payments accordingly
- to borrow more cheaply by taking advantage of opportunities for credit arbitrage.

A financial institution, such as a bank, might use swaps to hedge its exposures to a mismatch between its floating-rate assets and its floating-rate liabilities, or between its fixed-rate assets and its fixed-rate liabilities.

Changing the Fixed-Rate and Floating-Rate Mix

A company might wish to restructure its debt profile without having to borrow more or to repay existing loans.

Swaps have greatly improved the flexibility of the capital markets to end users. A company can alter its financial strategy cheaply and quickly as circumstances require. For example, a company might take over another company with a different debt profile. Swaps can be used in such a situation to readjust the fixed-rate/floating-rate debt mix to suit the company's preferred requirements.

However, an interest-rate swap alters the interest-rate market-risk profile of a company's debt. Paying a floating rate that is regularly adjusted in line with changes in short-term money-market interest rates, exposes a company to changes in economic and monetary conditions. For example, short-term rates might be raised by the monetary authorities as a measure to suppress inflation. In such circumstances, the interest cost of a company's debt could rise suddenly.

Example 1
A company has $100 million of debt. It pays a fixed rate of interest on $70 million and a variable rate on $30 million. Its management would prefer a mix of debt in which the ratio of fixed and floating rate debt is 50 : 50.

Analysis
Without repaying fixed-rate loans and taking on new floating-rate loans, the company could achieve its debt-restructuring objective by arranging a swap in which it is a receiver of fixed-rate interest and a payer of variable-rate interest on a notional principal of $20 million.

	Fixed rate $ million	**Floating rate** $ million
Debt structure	70	30
Swap	(20)	20
Net effect	50	50

A bank can use swaps to restructure the balance between its fixed and floating rate assets/liabilities, and so hedge its interest-rate exposures.

Example 2
A bank intends to obtain additional funding by issuing a ten-year bond. The additional funds will be used to increase the bank's lending activities that are mostly at a floating rate of interest.

Analysis
By issuing a fixed-rate bond to finance variable-rate lending activities, the bank will be exposed to a fall in interest rates. This exposure can be

hedged by a coupon swap in which the bank is a receiver of the fixed rate and pays the floating rate.

Issue bond: pay fixed rate	$- X\%$
Lend to customers at floating rate	$+ \text{LIBOR} + Y\%$
Swap: pay	$- \text{LIBOR}$
Swap: receive	$+ Z\%$
Net effect: profit	$+ (Z + Y - X)\%$

Inability to Borrow at a Fixed Rate

An important benefit of swaps to companies of weaker credit quality is the scope they offer for active interest-rate risk management.

It might be difficult for a company to raise fixed-rate funds in the primary borrowing markets, except perhaps at a very high rate. The difficulty could be because of

- market factors, or
- profit reasons.

Market Factors
Long-term borrowing at a rate fixed for the term of the loan is often difficult to obtain by small companies and companies with a weak credit rating. The principal source of fixed-rate finance is the bond market.

- Investors in the bond market cannot make careful credit decisions. They need to make quick and dirty decisions, relying on name recognition and credit ratings. Smaller and weaker companies have neither of these. There is a reasonably well-established junk bond market in the US, but the high-yield bond market in Europe is still very small.
- Many fund managers are not allowed to invest in unrated bonds or in bonds with a credit rating below a certain level, e.g. non-investment grade bonds. This drives up the cost of bond finance for lesser credits.
- The expenses and fees associated with a bond issue are high

and can make small-bond issues uneconomic.
- Small companies could try to borrow at a fixed rate in the bank lending market, but banks are reluctant to lend long term at a fixed rate, even to large companies.

Swaps provide small and weak companies with an alternative to obtaining fixed-rate funding by issuing bonds or borrowing at a fixed rate from banks. They can borrow at a floating rate and arrange a coupon swap in which they pay a fixed rate and receive the floating rate, thereby creating a synthetic fixed-rate debt.

Profit Reasons
Banks are exposed to the risk of adverse interest-rate movements on their fixed-rate lending, but not on their floating-rate lending that adjusts to prevailing market interest rates. If a bank lends at a fixed rate and interest rates go up, the bank's profit margins will be eroded because they obtain a large proportion of their funds as variable-rate deposits or loans. Banks therefore prefer variable-rate lending in order to contain their own interest-rate exposure, and may be reluctant to lend at a fixed rate except at a high margin.

Swaps can combine the elements of both coupon and basis swaps. For example it is common practise for companies seeking fixed-rate financing via a swap to issue commercial paper (CP) and swap into fixed rate against six-month dollar LIBOR.

Combining Coupon and Basis Swaps

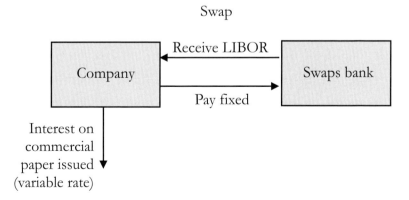

This creates a basis risk, because the spread between LIBOR and CP interest rates is not constant; therefore the amount received under the swap at LIBOR and the amount paid for the CP could differ over the term of the swap.

Anticipating Interest-Rate Changes

When a company borrows at a variable rate, it is exposed to the risk that the general level of interest rates and consequently that interest charges will rise. A company that borrows at a fixed rate is exposed to the risk of a fall in interest rates that would make variable-rate loans a cheaper and preferable method of funding.

A corporate treasurer might attempt to lower his/her company's long-term cost of debt by timing swap trades. For example, if he/she swaps into paying a fixed-rate before a rise in interest rates, higher interest costs will be avoided.

A judicious use of swaps can convert floating rate to fixed rate or vice versa as necessary to manage interest-rate exposures in line with a company's view of future interest-rate movements.

However, the drawback to this strategy is that it involves trying to buck the market, and expecting the banks, speculators and arbitrageurs who comprise most of the market, to get their interest expectations wrong.

Example 1
A company wishes to borrow for ten years at a fixed rate and intends to raise the funds in the near future. It takes the view, however, that long-term interest rates are near their cyclical peak.

Analysis
In order to obtain a favorable interest rate the company could borrow at a floating rate and swap into a fixed rate if and when rates fall. It could, of course, have borrowed at a fixed rate at the outset but then it would

be unable to benefit from the lower rates that the corporate treasurer expects at some time in the future. A swap would allow the company to obtain immediate funding, initially at a variable rate (anticipating a fall in interest rates) and ultimately at a cheaper fixed rate when the swap eventually is arranged.

Example 2
A company wishes to borrow £40 million at a fixed rate of interest. It could issue sterling bonds at a rate of 8.5% per annum. Its finance director believes that interest rates will fall in several months, but the company needs to raise funds now and cannot wait. A £40-million variable-rate loan could be obtained, with interest payable at six-month LIBOR plus 100 basis points. LIBOR currently is 8.0% per annum.

Analysis
Because the company believes that interest rates will soon fall, it might consider borrowing £40 million at LIBOR plus 100 bp. Interest for the first six months would be at 9.0% per annum, higher than for a fixed rate loan.

Suppose however that after six months or one year, LIBOR has fallen to 5.5% per annum, and the company believes rates are unlikely to fall much further. A swap bank might be willing to receive a fixed rate of 6.0% per annum against payments of LIBOR on a notional principal of £40 million. The effect of the swap would be:

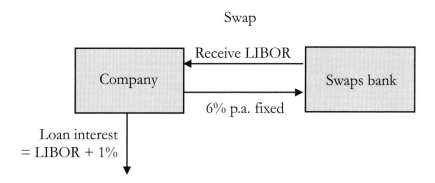

		%
Loan interest:	Pay	- (LIBOR + 1.0)
Swap:	Receive	+ LIBOR
	Pay	- 6.0
Net effect		- 7.0

The company has locked in a fixed rate of 7.0% per annum on its borrowings for the term of the swap. This is 1.5% per annum less than it would have paid by borrowing at a fixed rate from the outset.

Swaps and Risk-Taking
A decision to enter a swap agreement in anticipation of future interest-rate changes involves a large element of speculative risk. Swaps can be instruments for either hedging interest-rate exposures or for taking speculative risks on interest-rate movements. Clearly, if risks were to be taken with swaps transactions, it is essential they should be both affordable by the risk-taker and closely managed, otherwise an organization could incur large additional costs in the form of heavy losses, through its speculative activities.

Credit Arbitrage

A driving force behind the swaps market has been the ability of different borrowers to raise funds at different rates. Funding differentials between different borrowers have enabled swaps banks to create opportunities for their clients to borrow at very attractive rates.

Arbitrage is the process of exploiting price differences between two products or two markets to make an immediate and certain profit. Credit arbitrage opportunities arise when two organizations can each borrow in two different ways or markets, at interest rates that are comparatively better for one borrower in one market and for the other borrower in the other market.

Companies with better credit ratings will be able to obtain lower interest rates for borrowing in both the fixed-rate market (bond market) and the variable-rate market (loans market), compared with a company whose credit status is not as good. To exploit a credit arbitrage opportunity, each company must be able to borrow at a *comparatively* better rate in one market, but want funds in the other market.

For example, suppose that one company can raise fixed-rate funds comparatively cheaply in the bond market, but wants to borrow floating-rate funds in the eurocurrency market. At the same time, suppose that a company can raise funds at a comparatively better rate in the eurocurrency market than in the bond market, compared to the first company, but that this company wants to raise fixed-rate funds. A credit arbitrage opportunity could be exploited if the first company borrows fixed-rate funds by issuing bonds and the second company borrows floating-rate funds, and they arrange a coupon swap. As a result, both companies will achieve a lower net borrowing cost than if they borrowed directly in their preferred market (floating-rate dollars or fixed-rate dollars).

Example 1
Company A has a high credit rating and can borrow at a low fixed rate in the bond market, at 8% fixed for example, or can borrow from its bank at a variable rate of LIBOR plus 50 basis points. In contrast, Company B has a lower credit status, and can borrow in the bond market at only 10% fixed or at a variable rate of LIBOR plus 140 basis points.

Company A wants to borrow at a variable rate, and Company B wants to borrow at a fixed rate. The companies want to borrow the same amount of money, $20 million.

Analysis
In the fixed-rate borrowing market, Company B would have to pay 200 basis points (2%) more than Company A, but for variable rate borrowing, Company B would have to pay only 90 basis points more. Company B therefore can borrow at a comparatively better rate in the floating-rate funds market than in the fixed-rate market, compared to

Company A, by 110 basis points. This difference of 110 basis points creates scope for credit arbitrage through a swap.

- Company B, wanting to borrow fixed-rate funds, should borrow at a variable rate of LIBOR + 140 basis points, because it can borrow on comparatively better terms than in the bond market, compared with Company A.
- Company A, wanting to borrow variable-rate funds, should borrow at a fixed rate of 8.0%, because it can borrow on comparatively better terms than in the floating-rate market, compared with Company B.
- The two companies should arrange a swap, with Company A paying a fixed rate and company B receiving a fixed rate. The swap most probably would be arranged through a swaps bank that will take a turn for its services. The bank's profit can come from the 110 basis points of benefit to be obtained from the credit arbitrage.

The terms of the swap might be:

- Company A will receive a fixed rate of 7.90% and pay LIBOR.
- Company B will pay a fixed rate of 8.10% and receive LIBOR.

Credit Arbitrage

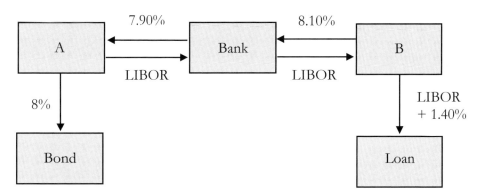

		Company A	Company B
		%	%
Borrowing cost:	Pay	- 8.00 fixed	- (LIBOR + 1.40)
Swap:	Receive	+ 7.90 fixed	+ LIBOR
	Pay	- LIBOR	- 8.10
Net effect		- (LIBOR + 0.10)	- 9.50

In this example, Company A has a net floating-rate borrowing cost that is 40 basis points lower than it would have obtained by borrowing directly at a variable rate of LIBOR plus 50 basis points.

Company B has a net fixed-rate borrowing cost that is 50 basis pints lower than it would have obtained by borrowing directly at a fixed rate of 10%.

The swaps bank takes a turn of 20 basis points, the difference between its fixed pay and receive rates in the swaps.

The total benefit for the two companies and the swaps bank is (40 + 50 + 20) 110 basis points, the amount of the credit arbitrage opportunity.

There is also a possibility that Company B might not have been able to borrow at all at a fixed rate, even at 10%, due to the poor credit status of the company or a lack of liquidity in the fixed-rate funds market (bond market) at the time. In such a situation, the only option available to Company B to obtain fixed-rate funding would have been to borrow at a variable rate and then swap into fixed-rate payments.

Example 2
PQ and RST each want to borrow £20 million for five years. PQ can borrow at 6.5% fixed or at LIBOR plus 50 basis points. RST, that has a lower credit rating, can borrow at 7.0% fixed or at LIBOR plus 125 basis points.

PQ wants to borrow at a fixed rate of interest and RST wants to borrow variable-rate funds.

Analysis
An interest-rate swap would provide an opportunity for credit arbitrage.

This is because RST can borrow at 50 basis points more than PQ at a fixed rate and at 75 basis points more at a variable rate. RST therefore has a comparative advantage of 25 basis points in the fixed-funds market, but wants to borrow at a variable rate. PQ has a comparative advantage of 25 basis points in the variable-funds market, but wants to borrow at a fixed rate.

The terms of a swap might be agreed as follows:

- PQ to borrow £20 million at a variable rate of LIBOR plus 50 basis points and RST to borrow £20 million at a fixed rate of 7.0%.
- The two companies to arrange a coupon swap with a swaps bank.
- RST to receive a fixed rate of 5.85% and pay LIBOR.
- PQ to pay a fixed rate of 5.90% and receive LIBOR.

Swap on Notional Principal of £20 million

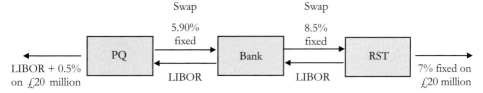

		PQ	RST
		%	%
Borrowing cost:	Pay	- (LIBOR + 0.50)	- 7.00
Swap:	Receive	+ LIBOR	+ 5.85
	Pay	- 5.90	- LIBOR
Net effect		- 6.40	- (LIBOR + 1.15)

The swaps bank will make a turn of five basis points, the difference between the fixed rate of 5.90% it receives from PQ and the fixed rate of 5.85% it pays to RST.

As a result of the swap, PQ has obtained fixed-rate borrowing of 6.40%, that is 0.10% lower than it could have obtained by borrowing directly at a fixed cost of 6.50%. RST has obtained net variable-rate borrowing costs of LIBOR plus 110 basis points, 10 basis points lower than it could have obtained by borrowing directly at a variable rate of LIBOR plus 125 basis points.

PS remains liable for its own variable-rate borrowing of £20 million, and RST remains liable for its fixed-rate borrowing of £20 million. The swap agreements do not affect their contractual obligations for their debts.

The turn of the swaps bank compensates the bank for

- arranging the swap, and
- accepting the credit risk. There is a risk that one of the companies will fail to carry out the terms of the swap agreement and make any due payments to the bank. A default by one of the companies would result in a loss for the bank.

For example, suppose that on a payment date for the swaps in this case, LIBOR is 6.25%. The swaps bank would be required to pay PQ interest at 35 basis points per annum for six months on £20 million (about £35,000), for the difference between LIBOR and the fixed rate receivable from PQ of 5.90%. The bank would be due to receive interest from RST at 40 basis points per annum for six months on £20 million (about £40,000), for the difference between LIBOR and the fixed rate of 5.85% payable to RST. If RST defaulted, the bank would still be required to make the payment to PQ, but would not receive the payment from RST. This would result in a loss for the bank.

Exercise 1
Attempt your own solution to this problem.

A company, Echo, has an existing floating-rate bank facility priced at LIBOR plus 125 basis points. It wants to alter its debt profile, and change from variable rate to fixed-rate debt, but does not want to pay above 7.5%.

Foxtrot, another company, can raise fixed-rate debt in the bond markets at 6%, or could borrow at LIBOR plus 25 basis points.

A bank negotiates a swap agreement with each company whereby Echo becomes a net payer of fixed interest at 7.35% and Foxtrot becomes a net payer at LIBOR minus five basis points.

How would this be arranged, and what would be the size of the turn for the swaps bank?

Solution
Foxtrot should borrow at a fixed rate of 6% that is 150 basis points below the maximum fixed rate that Echo wants to pay.

Echo is already borrowing at LIBOR plus 125 basis points, 100 basis points more than Foxtrot would have to pay.

There is a credit arbitrage difference of 50 basis points (150 − 100 basis points that can be shared out between Echo, Foxtrot and the swaps bank.

- Because Foxtrot will be a net payer of LIBOR minus five basis points that is 30 basis points lower than it would pay by borrowing directly at a floating rate, its share of the credit arbitrage profit will be 30 basis points.
- Because Echo will be a net payer of 7.35% that is 0.15% lower than the maximum it wants to pay, it will benefit by 15 basis points.
- The swaps bank will take a turn of five basis points, the profit remaining from 50 basis points after Echo and Foxtrot have taken their 15 and 30 basis points of profit respectively.

INTEREST-RATE SWAPS

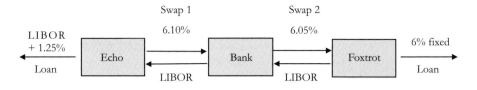

		Echo %	Foxtrot %
Borrowing cost:	Pay	- (LIBOR + 1.25)	- 6.00
Swap:	Receive	+ LIBOR	+ 6.05*
	Pay	- 6.10*	- LIBOR
Net effect		- 7.35	- (LIBOR – 0.50)

* These fixed pay and receive rates are balancing figures that you can calculate from the direct borrowing costs of Echo and Foxtrot, their net borrowing costs, and by assuming that the floating-rate payments in both the swaps will be at LIBOR.

The bank makes a turn of five basis points, the difference between the fixed rate of 6.10% paid by Echo and the fixed rate of 6.05% paid to Foxtrot.

Exercise 2

Credit arbitrage can be confusing. You might like to try one more exercise.

Gamma wants to obtain $20 million in fixed-rate funding for two years. It can borrow at a fixed rate of 6% or at a variable rate of LIBOR plus 80 basis points.

Delta wants to borrow a similar amount for the same term, but at a variable rate of interest. It can borrow at 5.4% fixed or at a variable rate of LIBOR plus 50 basis points.

Omega Bank will arrange a swap with each customer whereby

- Gamma and Delta share equally the profit from the credit arbitrage opportunity, after deducting the turn of Omega Bank

- Omega Bank takes a turn of five basis points.

Each swap will involve the receipt or payment of a fixed rate against LIBOR.

What are the terms of the swaps?

Solution

	Fixed-rate borrowing %	Variable-rate borrowing %
Gamma	6.00	LIBOR + 0.80
Delta	5.40	LIBOR + 0.50
Difference	0.60	0.30

The total benefit obtainable from credit arbitrage is 30 basis points (60 − 30). This will be shared as follows:

	Basis points
Omega Bank	5.0
Gamma	12.5
Delta	12.5
Total	30.0

Gamma wants to pay a fixed-rate and could borrow directly at a fixed rate of 6%. Its net cost with a swap has to be 12.5 basis points better than this, that is 5.875%. Similarly, Delta wants variable-rate funding, and could borrow directly at LIBOR plus 50 basis points. For a swap to give Delta a benefit of 12.5 basis points, its net interest cost must be LIBOR plus 37.5 basis points.

This can be achieved by:

		Gamma	**Delta**
		%	%
Borrowing cost:	Pay	- (LIBOR + 0.80)	- 5.400
Swap:	Receive	+ LIBOR	+ 5.025*
	Pay	- 5.075*	- LIBOR
Net effect		- 5.875	- (LIBOR + 0.375)

* These fixed pay and receive rates are balancing figures, that can be calculated from the direct borrowing costs of Gamma and Delta, their net borrowing costs, and the floating-rate payments in both the swaps that will be at LIBOR.

Gamma therefore will pay a fixed rate of 5.025% and receive LIBOR. Delta will receive a fixed rate of 5.075% and pay LIBOR. The bank makes a turn of five basis points, the difference between the fixed rate of 5.075% paid by Gamma and the fixed rate of 5.025% paid to Delta.

The Role of Banks

A bank plays one of two roles in the swaps market.

- It can be a counterparty to a swap in order to manage its own funding and interest-rate exposures.
- It can act as intermediary for two counterparties. This is how the swaps market developed.

The role of banks as swaps traders has developed in three stages: broking, warehousing and global risk management.

Broking
A bank arranges the introduction of two parties, showing them the idea for a swap, negotiating over several days and then closing the deal.

- The two parties might then sign an agreement with each other, and the bank takes an arrangement fee.
- The bank intermediates as principal for each side of the transaction, taking a profit from different pay and receive rates. The two parties may each not know the identity of the other. The bank uses its own balance sheet and assumes the credit (counterparty) risk for both sides of the swap.

Warehousing
Many clients do not want to wait for a bank to find another matching deal. Banks therefore started carrying out one leg of a swap and finding a matching leg some time later.

Global Risk Management
Warehousing swaps led banks to global risk management. All risks are

now put together in a large book of interest rate and currency instruments – swaps, options, FRAs, bonds etc. Banks do not hedge each individual deal, but look at the overall position, coping with mismatches between assets and liabilities as part of their natural business. Each deal they transact is priced against a public and highly liquid market.

A bank therefore can intermediate in a swap in either of two ways.

- First, it can arrange a direct swap between two parties, and act as broker for the transaction, charging an arrangement fee. In this situation, the bank does not act as a party in the swap transaction.
- It can act as a principal in two or more legs of a swap arrangement. In this situation, each customer of the bank wishing to arrange a swap enters into a swap agreement with the bank, and the bank accepts the credit risk (counterparty risk) of each party.

Normally swaps are not transacted directly between two non-bank companies. This is for several reasons:

- matching requirements
- credit risk
- tax positions.

Matching Requirements

In a direct-swap transaction, it is essential for the parties to have matching payments requirements, but in the opposite direction. In a coupon swap for example, one party must want to change from fixed to floating rate for a particular notional amount of principal and a particular term, with exchanges of payments on particular dates. The other party must want to swap exactly the same amounts at the same times and for the same term, but in the reverse direction from floating to fixed rate. Companies with opposite swap requirements rarely agree on the amount, term and simultaneous timing of a swap transaction. A financial director once said that he knew why he wanted to swap, but could never really understand why anyone wanted to swap the other way.

Even if there were two companies with equal and opposite requirements, a lack of awareness of each other's needs would prevent them getting together to arrange a swap.

Matching two sides of a swap exactly is very difficult, and to develop the market banks began to warehouse swaps, arranging one side of a transaction and waiting until a suitable customer came along for a swap in the other direction.

Specialist swap banks are in a better position to find companies with different requirements and match them, perhaps with multi-legged transactions involving three or more separate swaps. For example, if Customer A wishes to be a payer of fixed interest on $30 million, and Customer B and Customer C each wish to be a receiver of fixed interest on $20 million and $10 million respectively, all for a term of five years, an intermediary bank could match their requirements in a multi-legged swap arrangement consisting of three separate swap agreements.

Matching Requirements: Multi-Legged Swaps

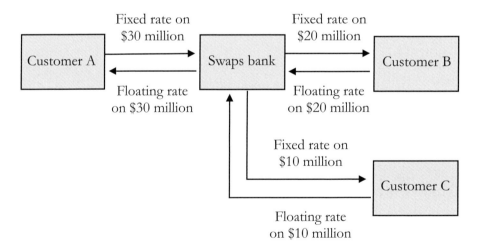

To the extent that it cannot match customer requirements exactly as to timing or amount, a swap bank would have an interest-rate exposure. However, swap banks usually are willing to have some such exposure in their swaps book that they could hedge with other instruments such as interest-rate futures.

Small Customers

Specialist swaps banks give small customers access to the use of swaps that they would be unable to achieve independently. For example, suppose that there is a demand from medium-sized corporates in Europe for fixed-rate funding, and the eurobond market is accessible only to larger corporates, banks and governments.

A swaps bank could issue eurobonds to raise fixed-rate funds, and swap these into variable-rate funds with a number of medium-sized companies. This is illustrated below.

Swaps Bank and Small Customers

From Bank	Amount	To Counterparty
Bond market	Borrow $100 million	→ Bank
Bank	$10 million	Counterparty A
Bank	$20 million	Counterparty B
Bank	$20 million	Counterparty C
Bank	$10 million	Counterparty D
Bank	$20 million	Counterparty E
Bank	Invest unused funds ($20 million)	Fixed rate investments e.g. Treasuries

The bank uses the swaps to obtain fixed-rate income to cover the cost of the interest on its bonds. Any surplus/unused funds could be put into fixed-rate investments, so as to avoid exposure to interest-rate risk. When other fixed-rate payers are found to transact further swaps, the bank could then hedge the new exposures by selling its fixed-rate investments.

Credit Risk

When two parties agree to a swap, they take on the risk that the other party might default. One of the functions of a swap bank is to minimize this risk by intermediating and acting as counterparty to both sides of the transaction. Companies arranging swaps normally will prefer a bank's credit risk to taking on credit risk for a non-bank company.

As party to a swap, the bank takes on a credit risk with the counterparty, whose remaining credit limit with the bank will be adjusted accordingly. For example, if a company arranges a swap with its bank on $50 million notional principal, the bank will adjust the company's remaining credit limit. Interest rate swaps normally are subject to a credit weighting of 1% to 2% for each year of the swap. For example, a $10 million swap for five years is likely to attract a credit weighting of 5% to 10% of the notional principal, and the bank will treat it as the equivalent of a loan of $0.5 million to $1 million.

Intermediate Banks

Some banks have a higher credit rating than others. For very large swaps, a highly rated bank or other financial institution such as an insurance company, might act as intermediary between a company and another swap bank, taking a small turn of perhaps just five to ten basis points (0.05-0.10%).

Although this turn is small in percentage terms, it provides useful income to an intermediary bank when applied to the large notional principal in the swap. The bank's function would be to provide greater assurance that the credit risk in the swap for the other counterparty is minimal.

Large Swaps: Intermediating Bank

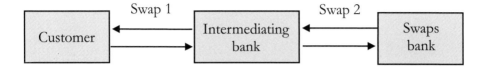

Tax Positions

The tax treatment of swaps varies from country to country. In particular, payments made from one party to the other under a swap arrangement might not be an allowable interest cost for tax purposes. For example, if a company with a variable-rate loan swaps into fixed-rate payments, tax would be allowable on the variable-rate loan interest, but might not be allowable on any net payments to the swap counterparty.

Swaps Book

Banks that deal in swaps do not wait for matching counterparties before agreeing to a swap transaction. For example, if a bank identifies a customer who wants to swap floating-rate dollars into fixed rate, it will not delay the transaction until it identifies another customer who wants to swap fixed-rate dollars into a floating rate. Instead, banks run a swaps book.

The book in effect is a running record of the bank's swap transactions, and in particular the swaps that do not have an exact match as to notional principal, payment dates and maturity.

A simplified example of a swaps book is shown opposite. The value of the transactions in this book will be continually marked-to-market and gains/losses reported on changes in their valuation.

Omega Bank Swaps Book: Dollar Swaps

Pay fixed rate

Maturity date	Amount ($ million)	Payments (annual/semi-annual)	Receive index	Pay %
Sept 24 2002	20	semi-annual	6m LIBOR	6.5
June 20 2003	25	annual	6m LIBOR	7.4
Aug 22 2003	15	semi-annual	6m LIBOR	7.5
Sept 27 2003	80	semi-annual	6m LIBOR	7.3
Nov 20 2003	50	semi-annual	6m LIBOR	7.6
Nov 29 2003	70	semi-annual	6m LIBOR	7.7
Apr 19 2005	25	semi-annual	6m LIBOR	7.7
July 11 2006	40	annual	6m LIBOR	7.6
July 27 2006	25	annual	6m LIBOR	7.9
Sept 11 2006	20	semi-annual	6m LIBOR	8.1
Total	370			

Receive Fixed Rate

Maturity date	Amount ($ million)	Payments (annual/semi-annual)	Receive index	Pay %
Aug 12 2002	10	annual	6m LIBOR	6.6
Oct 26 2002	20	semi-annual	6m LIBOR	7.4
Sept 11 2003	25	semi-annual	6m LIBOR	7.4
Nov 14 2003	20	annual	6m LIBOR	7.9
Nov 28 2003	60	annual	6m LIBOR	7.9
Apr 15 2004	100	semi-annual	6m LIBOR	7.8
Oct 14 2004	45	semi-annual	6m LIBOR	7.7
Nov 14 2005	30	semi-annual	6m LIBOR	7.8
Apr 15 2006	30	annual	6m LIBOR	8.1
Total	340			
Gross total	710			

Summary

By acting as principal to each counterparty in the swap, the bank reduces substantially the credit risk of the counterparty. Each counterparty is liable to the bank, not to the other counterparty. Also by acting as principal to each counterparty, the bank is able to keep the identity of each confidential.

The bank will charge each counterparty a fee for setting up and administering the swap. Normally it will do this by taking a turn, i.e. making a profit, on the periodic payments, receiving more from each counterparty than it pays to the other, giving it a profit perhaps of ten basis points (0.10%). This is also referred to as the bid-offer spread or just the spread.

Specialist banks employ swaps specialists whose job is to identify and arrange transactions with customers whose requirements might be satisfied by a swap. These give impetus to the market and probably swaps are initiated more frequently by swap banks than by the customer-counterparty.

The fact that swaps banks give indicative prices (rates) for fixed-rate swap payments means potential customers can compare the rates their banks are quoting, and makes for a more open market.

Swaps Rates

Swaps banks try to maintain a continuous two-way liquid market. This allows clients to enter into swaps at a time of their choosing and to reverse existing swaps if necessary. In a continuous and liquid swaps market, banks, or swaps brokers, must be able to quote rates for a range of maturities. For a company using swaps, it is important to understand how swaps rates might be quoted by a bank.

Swaps Rates: Pay Rates and Receive Rates

When a company is negotiating a swap with a bank, the bank will give an indicative fixed rate, reflecting current market rates of interest. The actual fixed rate will not be determined until the swap agreement is made. A bank's indicative fixed rates will vary according to the term of the swap and with market conditions.

It is usual to indicate rates for coupon swaps using three-month or six-month LIBOR as the standard index for the floating rate. This means that for this type of swap, dealers can indicate rates simply in terms of the fixed interest rates on the other side of the swap.

- There is a higher rate that the bank is willing to receive in return for making a variable-rate payment in a swap. This is the bid rate.
- There is a lower rate that the bank is willing to pay in return for receiving a variable-rate payment in a swap. This is the ask rate.

An illustrative example of what a swaps rate information screen might look like, showing rates for par swaps in several currencies, is shown below. Here, the bid rate is shown on the left and the ask rate is on the right. You may come across them shown the other way round.

Swaps Prices Screen

	US TREAS ACT/365	$ AMM ACT/360	EUR 30/360	CHF 30/360	£ ACT/365
2 YRS	T + 23-19	4.36-32	5.41-37	5.20-14	5.80-75
3 YRS	T + 31-27	5.07-03	5.09-04	4.88-82	6.10-05
4 YRS	T + 39-35	5.55-50	4.80-76	4.58-52	6.20-14
5 YRS	T + 32-28	5.95-90	4.66-62	4.48-42	6.38-32
7 YRS	T + 36-32	6.37-33	4.39-35	4.43-37	6.95-90
10 YRS	T + 37-34	6.75-71	4.29-25	4.31-25	7.02-97

dollar swap spreads (basis points over Treasury bond rates)

dollar outright swap rates

Notes
1. For the outright swap rates, the receive rate of the swaps bank is shown on the left and the lower (pay) rate is shown on the right in each column.
2. The information screen also shows the basis on which interest rate is calculated in each case (Actual/360, 30/360 and so on).

Swaps rates indicated on information screens or in the financial press are for standard transactions. Negotiated rates or spread sizes will differ when:

- a counterparty wants swap payments to times of its own choosing
- the transaction is very large or small
- the counterparty has either a very high or a poor credit status.

Example 1
A company with $20 million of variable-rate debt wishes to swap into fixed-rate payments. The debt has a further seven years to maturity. A bank is quoting rates for seven-year dollar swaps of 6.20-6.10%.

Analysis
The bank would be willing to arrange a seven-year swap during which the company is a payer at a fixed rate of 6.20% and a receiver of LIBOR, with notional principal of $20 million and six-monthly payment intervals.

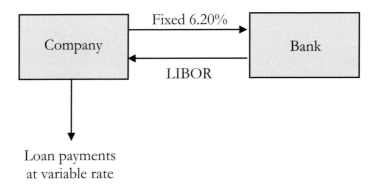

Example 2
A company with $30 million of five-year fixed-rate debt wants to swap into variable rate. A bank is quoting rates for five-year dollar swaps of 5.90-5.80%.

Analysis
The bank would be willing to arrange a swap in which the company is a receiver of fixed-rate payments at 5.80% and a payer at a variable rate of six-month dollar LIBOR, with notional principal of $30 million.

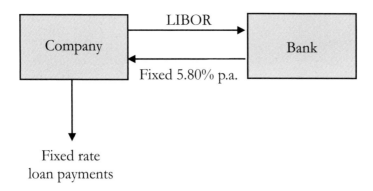

Example 3
The following pay rates and receive rates might be quoted for dollar coupon swaps.

Term (years)	Receive rate %	Pay rate %
2	5.96	5.91
3	6.00	5.95
4	6.06	6.01
5	6.12	6.07
7	6.24	6.19
10	6.34	6.29

Analysis
The lower rate is the rate that the banks will pay against six-month LIBOR. The higher rate is the fixed rate that the bank would want to receive against payments at six-month LIBOR. If Alpha Corporation wanted to arrange a five-year swap in which it is a payer of fixed-rate interest against LIBOR, the bank would want a rate of 6.12%. Similarly if Beta Corporation wished to arrange a ten-year swap in which it is a receiver of fixed interest against LIBOR, the bank would offer a fixed rate of 6.29%, the bank's pay rate.

Swap Spreads

Instead of quoting an outright fixed rate for swaps, a bank might quote rates in relation to another fixed-rate financial instrument that acts as a benchmark, typically the rate of interest on benchmark fixed-rate government bonds with the same maturity. For dollar swaps, the benchmark would be the rate for the most liquid Treasury note or bond nearest in maturity to the swap. For example, swap rates might be quoted for a five-year dollar swap at a spread above a five-year Treasury-note rate.

Example
A company wishes to arrange a three-year swap on a notional principal amount of $20 million, in which it is a fixed-rate payer. A bank quotes a spread of 70-64.

The bank's spread is quoted in basis points above the three-year Treasury-note rate. At this rate a swap could be arranged in which the company pays 70 basis points above 5.80%, that is a fixed rate of 6.50%, against receipt of six-month LIBOR.

The table opposite shows swap pay and receive rates for fixed sterling for a range of swap maturities. The figures are illustrative only. A bank quotes receive and pay spreads, and the appropriate spread would be added to the bond yield when the swap is negotiated to derive the fixed pay rate or receive rate for the term of the swap. The bank would quote the spread rather than the full swap rate because the full fixed rate payable or receivable will not be determined until the swap agreement is made. When the swap agreement is made, the agreed spread will be added to whatever the benchmark government bond rate happens to be at the time, to obtain the swap rate payable or receivable.

SWAPS RATES

Term (years)	Sterling bond yield		Swap spread		Swap rate	
	Bid (A)	Offer (B)	Receive (C)	Pay (D)	Receive (A) + (D)	Pay (B) + (C)
2	5.80	5.75	0.20	0.17	6.00	5.92
3	6.05	6.00	0.25	0.22	6.30	6.22
4	6.30	6.25	0.28	0.24	6.58	6.49
5	6.52	6.47	0.36	0.31	6.88	6.78
7	6.82	6.77	0.45	0.40	7.27	7.17
10	7.19	7.14	0.54	0.48	7.73	7.62

Swap rates for sterling take the bid-offer spread on government bond yields into account. This is not the case with dollar swaps, because the dollar swaps market is much more liquid. Dollar swap spreads are added to the *mid-market yields*, i.e. the yield half-way between the bid and offer yields. A sample screen is shown below.

Swaps up to ten years' maturity are shown in this illustrative example. In practise, swap rates for dollar swaps are quoted up to 30 years.

Maturity	Yield	Yld Mid	Spread	sa 30/360
2Y	7.592-587	7.589	48/46	8.069-8.049
3Y	7.742-730	7.736	42/40	8.156-8.136
4Y	7.782-770	7.776	40/38	8.176-8.156
5Y	7.818-811	7.814	38/36	8.194-8.174
6Y	7.826-819	7.823	39/37	8.213-8.193
7Y	7.837-829	7.833	39/37	8.223-8.203
8Y	7.845-837	7.841	39/37	8.231-8.211
9Y	7.854-846	7.850	39/37	8.240-8.220
10Y	7.865-856	7.860	39/37	8.250-8.230

Using these rates, if a client negotiates a five-year swap in which he/she is a receiver of fixed-rate interest against LIBOR, the bank (as payer of fixed interest) would pay 8.174% per annum in return for receiving LIBOR. This is the mid yield on the benchmark five-year Treasury bond (7.814%) plus the bank's spread for the pay rate that is 0.360%.

Exercise

The five-year Treasury note rate is 5.42%. A company wishes to arrange a five-year swap in which it pays variable rate and receives fixed rate. A bank quotes a spread for five-year swaps of 88-82. What would be the fixed-rate payment in the swap?

Solution

The bank will pay a fixed rate of 6.24% (5.42% + 0.82%).

Swap spreads are used extensively for quoting rates for dollar swaps. Although Treasury note yields vary continually in the market, swap spreads generally are quite stable, depending on supply and demand in the market. Rates for swaps in other currencies also are often quoted as a spread rather than as an outright fixed rate.

Spread Size

The size of the spread above the government bond yield is determined by supply and demand for swaps. Swap spreads will increase or fall according to how strong or weak demand is for swaps.

A bank could set a target spread between its pay and receive rates that represents its turn. This spread is likely to increase with the tenor of the swap. For example, a bank's target spread might be:

Swap term years	Spread (receive/pay rates) basis points
2	2
3	3
5	4
10	6

Price Changes: Market-Making in Swaps

Swap prices change in response to supply and demand. A bank that is a market maker in swaps will keep its spreads at a stable level above the benchmark rate – Treasury-note rate or gilts rate etc. – provided that customer demand to pay fixed rate matches the demand from other customers to pay variable rate. When demand for either variable-rate or fixed-rate payments predominates, the bank's swaps trader will adjust prices accordingly.

Example

A swaps trader in a bank has been quoting a spread of 90-80 on five-year dollar swaps that is comparable with other prices in the market. Recently, however, the trader has arranged several swaps in which the customer as counterparty is a payer of a fixed rate. Now the aim is to encourage more business where the customer is a variable-rate payer in order to balance the swaps book.

Analysis

To attract interest from more customers wishing to be variable-rate payers, the swaps trader should raise the fixed rate that the bank is willing to pay. To discourage business with customers wishing to be fixed-rate payers, the bank also should raise the rate that it would wish to receive. The trader therefore might adjust the bank's spreads to 93-83 basis points.

Fixed and Floating-Rate Quotations

A fixed swap rate is quoted in one of four ways, to indicate semi-annual or annual payments (sa or pa), and whether settlement is on a bond basis or a money-market basis. The four ways of quoting a fixed rate are:

- *pab* – annual interest payments settled on a bond basis. This is the most common method of quotation for fixed rates
- *pamm* – annual interest payments settled on a money-market basis
- *sab* – semi-annual interest payments settled on a bond basis
- *samm* – semi-annual interest payments settled on a money-market basis.

Sa and pa

When an interest rate is quoted on a semi-annual basis, it means interest is payable every six months at half the coupon rate. For example, 10% sa means that interest is payable at 5% of the notional principal every six months. Similarly, 8% sa means interest payable six-monthly at 4% of the notional principal. Interest rates can be converted from a semi-annual basis to an equivalent annual (pa) basis using the formula:

$$\text{pa basis} = S + [(\tfrac{1}{2} \text{ of } S)^2 \div 100]$$

where S is the sa rate of interest.

Similarly, to convert from a pa basis to an sa basis, the formula is

$$\text{sa basis} = 200 \left[\sqrt{\left(1 + \frac{P}{100}\right)} - 1 \right]$$

where P is the pa rate of interest.

Examples
We can convert 10% sa and 8% sa to a pa basis as follows:

sa basis	pa basis	
10% sa	$10 + [5^2 \div 100]$	= 10.25%
8% sa	$8 + [4^2 \div 100]$	= 8.16%

We can convert 7% pa basis to an sa basis as follows:

pa basis	sa basis	
7% pa	$200 [\sqrt{1.07} - 1]$	= 200 (0.0344)
	= 6.88%.	

It should be noted that when a fixed-rate swap rate is quoted on a semi-annual basis, the equivalent pa basis is higher. For example, 8% on a semi-annual basis means 4% every six months. On an annual basis, this is 8.16% (see example above). This means that interest payable at 8% sa basis will be more than interest at 8% pa basis, i.e. interest paid at 8% annually.

Bond Basis and Money-Market Basis (Dollar Rates)
Dollar-interest rates quoted on a bond basis assume a 365-day year, and

interest is calculated on an Actual/365 day basis. In contrast, dollar rates quoted on a money-market basis assume a 360-day year, and interest is calculated on an Actual/360 day basis.

To compare fixed rates payable in a swap (bond basis) and floating rates payable (money-market basis), it is necessary either to:

- convert the fixed rate from a fixed-rate basis to an equivalent money-market basis, or
- convert the money-market rate from a money-market basis to an equivalent bond basis.

To convert from a bond basis to a money-market basis, it is necessary to multiply by a factor of 360/365. To convert from a money-market basis to a bond basis, it is necessary to multiply by a factor of 365/360.

Money-market basis	=	Bond basis x 360/365
Bond basis	=	Money-market basis x 365/360

Example
A swap price is quoted as 5.80% samm. The bond basis equivalent of this would be 5.80% x 365/360 = 5.88% sab.

Day-Count Conventions
The conversion between money market and bond day-count conventions will depend on the conventions used in each market in any given currency.

For example, as mentioned earlier, money markets assume 360 interest-earning days in the year. The Treasury bond market assumes 365 days in the year, roughly speaking.

Users of swaps should be aware of the exact basis on which the swap rates are quoted, and adjust these as necessary for comparison with other interest rates, such as target interest costs that a swap user is trying to achieve. For example, if a company issues fixed-rate *bonds* on which interest is paid *every six months*, and wishes to swap the fixed-rate payments into floating-rate payments, it should look at the fixed-rate receipts from the swap on an *sab* basis, to establish its overall interest costs.

Matched Swap Payments

Swap prices (for par swaps) are fixed rates quoted by a bank on the assumption that the floating-rate payments will be at a benchmark rate of interest, such as six-month LIBOR flat. However, a company might prefer to arrange a liability swap in which the swap payments received match exactly the company's payment obligations under a loan agreement. This could mean swap payments above or below the LIBOR rate and fixed-rate payments at a rate above or below the bank's quoted prices.

Negotiating Matched Payments

A company must first establish the amount and timing of its loan payments. It should then ask for a swap arrangement in which it receives these amounts at the required times. The swap bank will specify the payments it would require in exchange. The three steps in negotiating matched payments are:

- determine the cash payments on the loan
- neutralize or match these cash payments with swap receipts
- establish the required swap payments.

Example 1
Victor is a company with a triple-A credit rating, and Tango is a company with a lower, single-A rating. They can borrow for five years at the following rates.

	Fixed	Floating
Victor	7% p.a.	6-month LIBOR + 10 basis points
Tango	9% p.a.	6-month LIBOR + 60 basis points

Victor would like to borrow $100 million for five years at a floating rate with interest payable six-monthly, and Tango would like to borrow the same amount for the same maturity, but at a fixed rate, with interest payable annually. A swaps bank identifies an opportunity for credit arbitrage, and indicates a swap price of 7.90-7.80% (pa bond basis).

Both companies ask the bank to arrange a swap. Victor might borrow $100 million at 7% per annum by issuing bonds, with interest payable annually for example, and swap into floating rate. Tango would borrow $100 million at LIBOR plus 0.60% and swap into fixed rate with interest payable annually. Each company has specified that it would like to receive payments under the swap that match exactly its loan-payment obligations.

Analysis
Each leg of the swap must be considered separately.

Victor
Suppose that Victor did not want to match its loan payments exactly, and arranged a swap in which it received 7.80% fixed (pa bond basis) against six-month dollar LIBOR.

Matching Payment Obligations

FIXED-RATE LOAN

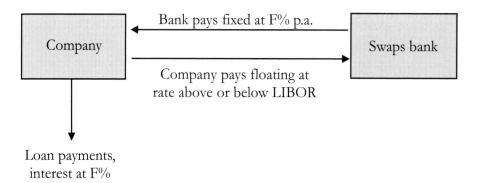

Loan payments, interest at F%

VARIABLE-RATE LOAN

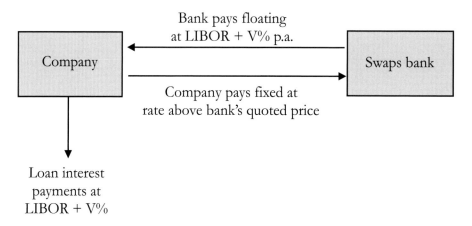

Loan interest payments at LIBOR + V%

The cash flows would be:

	Payments on bond at 7%	Swap payments Receive at 7.8%	Pay
Year	$ million	$ million	$ million
1	(7.0)	+ 7.8 p.a.	(LIBOR)
2	(7.0)	+ 7.8 p.a.	(LIBOR)
3	(7.0)	+ 7.8 p.a.	(LIBOR)
4	(7.0)	+ 7.8 p.a.	(LIBOR)
5	(7.0)	+ 7.8 p.a.	(LIBOR)

———————————————————————————————— MATCHED SWAP PAYMENTS ——————

Victor would pay LIBOR on the swap, and in addition make a profit of $800,000 each year as the surplus of swap receipts over interest paid on the bonds.

Victor prefers, however, to match swap receipts with payments exactly, and wants a swap in which it is a receiver of a fixed $7 million each year. This can be arranged, with Victor paying a floating rate *below* LIBOR instead of receiving the surplus $800,000 each year.

The floating-rate payments will be at six-month LIBOR minus the difference between the swap rate received (7.0% per annum bond basis) and the quoted swap rate (7.8% pab). The difference is adjusted from a bond basis to a money-market basis because LIBOR rates are quoted on a money-market basis.

pa bond basis		sa bond basis	samm basis
7.8%	$200\left[\sqrt{\left(1 + \dfrac{7.8}{100}\right)} - 1\right] = 7.6536\%$		
7.0%	$200\left[\sqrt{\left(1 + \dfrac{7.0}{100}\right)} - 1\right] = 6.8816\%$		
Difference		0.7720%	$\times \dfrac{360}{365} = 0.7610$

The difference on a samm basis is the amount below LIBOR that would be payable as the floating rate of interest in a coupon swap for 7.0% pab fixed.

Victor therefore would pay floating rate at six-month LIBOR minus 76.10 basis points and receive fixed 7.0%, with floating swap payments every six months and fixed payments annually.

Tango

Tango has borrowed $100 million and is paying a variable rate of six-month LIBOR plus 0.60%. It wishes to swap into fixed-rate payments, and would like to receive floating rate at LIBOR plus 0.60%. Because it will receive interest at a rate above LIBOR, it must pay the swap bank a higher rate than the quoted 7.90%.

The excess over 7.90% payable is the rate above LIBOR received (0.60%) adjusted from LIBOR semi-annual money-market basis to an annual bond basis (pab).

Excess over LIBOR

samm	sab	pab
$0.6000 \left(\times \dfrac{365}{360} \right)$	$0.6083 + \left[\left(\dfrac{0.6083}{2} \right)^2 \div 100 \right]$	0.6092

The excess payable is 0.6092%, and Tango therefore will pay a fixed rate annually of 8.5092% pab.

The swaps for both Victor and Tango are summarized in the table below.

Year	End of	Victor Payment on bonds $ million	Swap payments Fixed $ million	Swap payments Floating $ million
1	First 6 months			(LIBOR – 76.10 bp)
	Second 6 months	(7.0)	7.0	(LIBOR – 76.10 bp)
2	First 6 months			(LIBOR – 76.10 bp)
	Second 6 months	(7.0)	7.0	(LIBOR – 76.10 bp)
3	First 6 months			(LIBOR – 76.10 bp)
	Second 6 months	(7.0)	7.0	(LIBOR – 76.10 bp)
4	First 6 months			(LIBOR – 76.10 bp)
	Second 6 months	(7.0)	7.0	(LIBOR – 76.10 bp)
5	First 6 months			(LIBOR – 76.10 bp)
	Second 6 months	(7.0)	7.0	(LIBOR – 76.10 bp)
5	Redeem bonds	(100.0)		

MATCHED SWAP PAYMENTS

Year	End of	Tango Payment on loan $ million	Swap payments Floating $ million	Swap payments Fixed $ million
1	First 6 months	(LIBOR + 60 bp)	LIBOR + 60 bp	
	Second 6 months	(LIBOR + 60 bp)	LIBOR + 60 bp	8.5092
2	First 6 months	(LIBOR + 60 bp)	LIBOR + 60 bp	
	Second 6 months	(LIBOR + 60 bp)	LIBOR + 60 bp	8.5092
3	First 6 months	(LIBOR + 60 bp)	LIBOR + 60 bp	
	Second 6 months	(LIBOR + 60 bp)	LIBOR + 60 bp	8.5092
4	First 6 months	(LIBOR + 60 bp)	LIBOR + 60 bp	
	Second 6 months	(LIBOR + 60 bp)	LIBOR + 60 bp	8.5092
5	First 6 months	(LIBOR + 60 bp)	LIBOR + 60 bp	
	Second 6 months	(LIBOR + 60 bp)	LIBOR + 60 bp	8.5092
5	Repay loan	(100.0)		

Example 2

You might like to try to work out your own solution to the following problem before checking the analysis provided.

Baker is a multinational company with a sterling debt of $50 million on which interest is payable annually at a fixed rate of 7%. The debt has three years left to maturity, and the company, expecting interest rates to fall, would like to swap into floating-rate payments with interest payable six-monthly. A swaps bank quotes prices of 6.10-6.00% (semi-annual bond basis). Baker would like swap receipts to match exactly the 12-monthly interest-rate payments on its debt.

What floating rate would Baker pay under the swap agreement?

Analysis

Baker wishes to receive fixed payments of $3.5 million (7% of $50 million) on an annual basis. The swaps bank's quoted rate is 6.00% on a semi-annual bond basis. Baker wishes to receive fixed payments at 7%, that is above the coupon rate of the swaps bank, therefore it must pay a floating rate above LIBOR.

The following adjustments are required.

First, we must convert the 7% annual payment on the fixed-rate debt to a semi-annual bond basis:

$$\text{Semi-annual bond basis} = 200\left[\sqrt{\left(1 + \frac{7}{100}\right)} - 1\right] = 6.8816.$$

The final part of the calculation is as follows.

	pab	sab	samm
Baker wants to receive (fixed)	7.00% =	6.8816%	
Bank swap rate		6.0000%	
Difference		0.8816%	$= \times \left(\dfrac{360}{365}\right)$
			= 0.8695

Baker will receive 7% pab and will pay six-month LIBOR plus 86.95 basis points, possibly rounded up to 87 basis points because it is unlikely that a swaps bank will quote fractions of a basis point.

Summary

Swap receipts can be tailored to the specific requirements of a customer, and a swaps bank will adjust its rates for the swaps payment accordingly.

Asset Swaps

So far in this book, interest-rate swaps have been described from the starting point of a customer with a debt (liability) who wishes to change from fixed-rate payments to floating rate or vice versa. An asset swap or asset-based swap, is a swap that is similar to a liability swap but is used for a different purpose.

An asset swap starts attached to an asset, e.g. an investment, rather than a liability, and is used to exchange a fixed-rate income stream to a floating-rate income stream, or vice versa. Whereas liability swaps are used by borrowers, asset swaps are used by investors.

Why use Asset Swaps?

Asset swaps usually are arranged to create synthetic floating-rate assets, by combining:

- the purchase of a fixed-rate bond with
- an asset swap, whereby the bond holder pays over the bond income to a swaps bank, and receives a (negotiated) spread over LIBOR.

Asset swaps might be arranged by financial institutions such as Japanese regional banks, German regional banks and mutual funds, whose own liabilities are predominantly floating-rate debt finance. An asset swap enables institutions like this to hedge their interest-rate exposures by matching their floating-rate liabilities with synthetic floating-rate assets.

Example 1
A large multinational company is issuing a seven-year dollar bond at par with a coupon rate of 5% per annum. An investment bank, Jay Bank, has been approached about the possibility of buying $100 million of the bonds at par value.

Jay Bank will buy the bonds, but only if it could receive interest at six-month dollar LIBOR plus 25 basis points, rather than at 8% fixed.

Analysis
A seven-year swap could be arranged whereby Jay Bank buys $100 million of bonds, and arranges a swap in which it pays 5% fixed (sab basis) and receives six-month LIBOR plus 25 basis points on notional principal of $100 million.

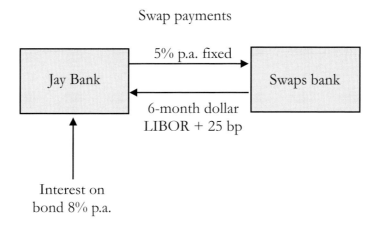

This is the most common form of asset swap. In practise, Jay Bank would not agree to the bond purchase and swap if it could invest $100 million directly in a variable-rate investment with the same risk profile, earning more than six-month LIBOR plus 25 basis points. This swap would be attractive, however, if six-month LIBOR plus 25 basis points is the best yield that Jay Bank could obtain for its money.

Example 2
ABC plc, a large blue-chip UK public company, has invested some

surplus funds in £25 million of floating-rate notes (FRNs), that pay LIBOR plus 0.50%. The company's funding includes £25 million of fixed-rate bonds, on which the interest rate is 6%. ABC's finance director would like to cover the company's bond payments by locking in a fixed-interest rate for its FRNs. In other words, the company wants to hedge its interest-rate risk by securing a guaranteed income from its FRN investments that it can use to cover the costs of the interest payments on its bonds.

The swaps desk of a bank quotes a fixed swap rate of 6.30 – 6.15% (semi-annual bond basis) against six-month LIBOR.

CURRENT POSITION

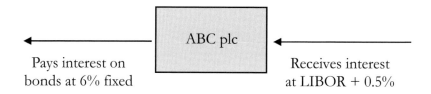

Pays interest on bonds at 6% fixed   Receives interest at LIBOR + 0.5%

DESIRED POSITION

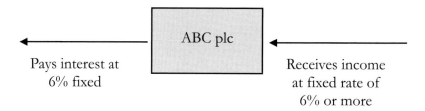

Pays interest at 6% fixed   Receives income at fixed rate of 6% or more

Analysis
ABC plc can lock in interest-rate income for its assets as follows:

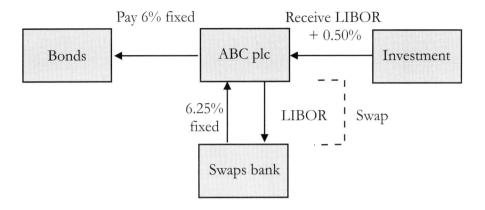

ABC plc's position is now:

	%
Income from FRN investment	LIBOR + 0.50
Swap: pay	− LIBOR
Swap: receive	+ 6.25
Bond: interest payable	− 6.00
Net position: surplus	+ 0.75

This example illustrates a swap from floating to fixed-rate income. Asset swaps equally can be arranged the other way round, from fixed to floating-rate income.

Other Features of Asset Swaps

Investors often prefer asset swaps where:

- the assets do not have any accrued interest
- the assets are priced at par
- the coupon paid on the asset is equal to the coupon paid through the swap.

If an asset swap is arranged with the purchase of newly issued investments, e.g. bonds, the assets would not have any accrued interest and could have a par value at the time of issue. If an asset swap is arranged for an investment in securities that are already in issue, there will be some accrued interest on the bonds when the swap is arranged. In addition, the securities probably will not be priced at par, but will have a market price above or below par.

When arranging a swap, this problem can be overcome by means of an adjusting payment by one party to the swap to the other, as compensation for the accrued interest and the premium or discount to par value of the securities.

Example
Suppose an investor buys 8% bonds with a nominal value of $50 million and a current market price of 96.0 ($48 million), and with 4.85 years left to redemption. Accrued interest at the time of purchase is $600,000. The investor negotiates a swap with a bank so as to swap from fixed-rate income to floating-rate income.

Analysis
The current price of the bond is below par, indicating that the coupon rate of 8% is below the current market rate payable on bonds of that type and maturity.

The investor buys the bonds for $48 million (at 96.00) plus accrued interest of $600,000.

Let's suppose that the investor wants to arrange a swap where the resulting synthetic asset has no accrued interest and is valued at par.

- The swaps bank could make an up-front payment of $600,000 to compensate the investor for having to pay the accrued interest when buying the bonds.
- The discount of the bond's current market price to par ($2 million) can be compensated by an up-front payment by the investor to the swaps bank. In addition, an adjustment to the floating-rate payment in the swap also will be necessary. Because the bonds are valued below par, the investor is receiving a coupon on the bonds that is below the current

market rate, but paying a market rate in the swap. The swaps bank therefore will pay a floating rate of LIBOR plus a margin throughout the term of the swap.

Up-Front Compensation Payment

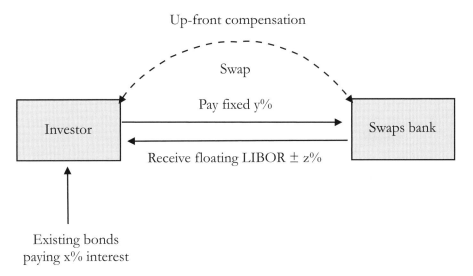

As a result, the investor will recover the $2 million up-front payment in the form of higher floating-rate receipts over the term of the swap.

Premium Swaps/Discount Swaps

Investors in asset swaps usually want the fixed payments in the swap to be at the same rate as the fixed coupon on the asset (bonds). The problem can be overcome by arranging a swap in which the two rates are the same. As a result, the swap will be priced at an off-market rate. These swaps are called premium swaps or discount swaps.

The party in the swap that is at a disadvantage by paying or receiving the off-market rate is compensated by either:

- a cash payment from the other party, usually paid up-front at the start of the swap, or

- an adjustment to the floating-interest rate in the swap, by adding or subtracting a margin in basis points from the floating-rate benchmark rate.

The amount of compensation payable should have a present value equal to the difference between:

- the present value of the fixed payments at the agreed (coupon) rate in the swap agreement, and
- the present value of the fixed payments at the current market rate for swaps.

Premium/Discount Swaps

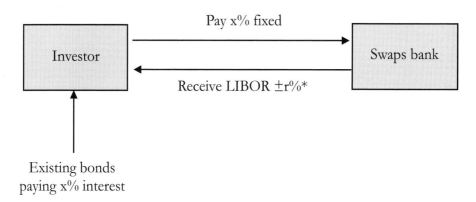

* Floating rate = LIBOR plus or minus a margin, in basis points.

Alternatively, there is an up-front payment of compensation from one party in the swap to the other, to reflect the off-market pricing of the fixed rate in the swap.

Example
It may be helpful to develop the previous example further. An investor buys bonds with a $50-million nominal value, paying a coupon of 8%. The purchase price is $48.0 million (96.00). The bonds have 4.85 years left to redemption. Accrued interest on the bonds at the time the swap is arranged amounts to $600,000.

The swaps bank receives a net up-front payment of $1.4 million. This is the $2 million by which the market value of the bonds ($48 million) is below par value ($50 million), less the accrued interest of $600,000. Subsequently the swaps bank will receive payments under the swap to match the payments on the bonds. Assuming an annual coupon on the bonds, these payments will be:

Year	Swap payments $ million
0	1.4
0.85	4.0
1.85	4.0
2.85	4.0
3.85	4.0
4.85	4.0

(The annual interest payments, after 0.85 years and then annually thereafter, amount to 8% on $50 million = $4 million.)

The swaps bank will value these receipts, using discounted cash flow, to derive their present value to the bank. For example, if the bank wished to receive a yield of 8.5% per annum, these cash flows would be discounted at 8.5% to obtain their present value. In this example, the present value of the cash flows, discounted at 8.5%, is $16.8 million (workings are not shown).

Receiving cash flows over the next 4.85 years with a present value of $16.8 million is equivalent to receiving a fixed coupon stream of about $4.365 million per annum over 4.85 years. (Again, the workings are not shown.) An annual fixed coupon stream of $4.365 million on bonds with a nominal value of $50 million represents 8.73% per annum. If the swaps bank is receiving 8.73% per annum, but wants to receive only 8.5%, it can afford to pay the swap counterparty a floating rate in excess of LIBOR.

	%
Equivalent receipt	8.73
Required yield	8.50
Difference	0.23

The bank therefore will pay the other party a floating rate of about LIBOR + 23 basis points. There will be some adjustment to allow for the different interest-rate bases between the fixed and floating-rate payments.

In this example we have assumed a constant interest rate over the full term of the swap. In reality, the yield curve is rarely if ever perfectly flat, and a constant discount rate over the term of the swap will be inappropriate. Accuracy requires that the swaps bank should calculate the present value of each fixed-interest receipt in the swap separately, using a different yield/discount rate for each. The appropriate discount rate for each individual cash flow is the zero coupon swap rate appropriate to the timing of that cash flow. Zero coupon rates are explained in the appendix to this book.

Non-Generic Swaps

The most common type of interest-rate swap is the plain vanilla coupon swap, but as the swaps market has evolved, various non-generic swaps have been introduced to the market. Three are described in this chapter,

- forward start swaps
- amortizing swaps
- LIBOR in arrears swaps.

Basis swaps, another type of non-generic swap, were described in Chapter 2 and premium swaps and discount swaps were described in Chapter 7.

The derivatives markets are very innovative, and non-generic swaps with other non-standard features have been transacted.

Forward-Start Swaps

An interest-rate swap usually has a spot start date. Spot start means two business days after the transaction is made. Swaps can be arranged, however, involving a later start date than spot. For example, a three-year swap can be arranged, to start in six months' time. These swaps are called forward-start swaps.

The start date for the swap could be up to two or three years from the date the swap transaction is made. However, most forward-start swaps are bond-related. One reason for the delayed swap start is to match the interest periods of the underlying transaction, such as the interest payments on bonds, with the interest periods of the swap.

If a swap has a delay in the start date, the swaps bank will alter its fixed-rate price. The adjustment is calculated by taking the difference between the bank's funding cost for the period of the delay to the start of the swap, and the swap rate for the period of the swap.

If the short-term interest rates are lower than long-term rates, a swaps bank will be prepared to pay a higher fixed rate and would wish to receive a higher fixed rate for a forward-start swap than for a swap starting immediately. Similarly, if short-term rates are higher than long-term rates, a swaps bank would quote lower fixed pay and receive rates for a forward-start swap.

Example
A five-year swap has a delayed start of one month. The five-year swap rate is 6.75% per annum and the six-year swap rate is 6.87%. The funding cost of the swaps bank for one month is 4.75% per annum.

Analysis
The interest rate differential is 2% per annum or 0.1666% (2 ÷ 12) for one month. This differential could be settled by a one-off payment to the swaps bank by the customer, or from the bank to the customer at the start of the deal. However, in practise the cost or benefit is spread over the term of the swap by adjusting the fixed rate in the swap.

An approximate method of calculation is as follows:

- Estimate the interest rate for a term of five years and one month, the length of time to the end of the swap. We can estimate this rate by interpolating between the five-year and the six-year swap rates.

	%
Six-year rate	6.87
Five-year rate	6.75
Difference	+ 0.12
Difference per month (÷ 12)	+ 0.01
Estimated rate for 5 yrs 1 month (6.75 + 0.01)	6.76

- Find the difference between this rate and the one-month funding rate.

	%
Swap rate for 5 yrs 1 month	6.76
One-month funding rate	4.75
Difference	2.01

- This difference is stated at an annual rate of interest. The swap has a one-month forward start; therefore we convert this annual cost difference to a one-month equivalent. Here, the value is approximated by dividing the annual rate by 12.

    $2.01/12 = 0.17\%$ for one month (approximately)

- Amortize this cost over the five-year life of the swap. This gives an annual equivalent of 0.04% per annum for five years (workings not shown).

In this example, there would be an adjustment of about four basis points (0.04%). If the swaps bank is quoting rates for a five-year swap of 6.80-6.70%, the bank would be prepared to pay 6.74% (6.70% plus four basis points) or to receive 6.84% (6.80% plus four basis points) for a five-year swap with a one-month forward start. (Note: these calculations are approximate and simplified in order to make the explanation clearer. An accurate calculation of forward start rates would use zero coupon swap rates that are described in the Appendix.)

Amortizing Swaps

A company might have a loan on which the principal is being repaid gradually (an amortizing loan). A swap can be arranged whereby the payments are decreased over time to reflect reductions in the outstanding balance on the loan.

Example
A company has a loan of $30 million for which the principal will be

repaid in three equal annual instalments. Interest is fixed at 7% per annum, with annual payments. The company wishes to swap into variable-rate payments. A swaps bank's quoted prices are:

Term of swap	Swaps rates %
1 year	6.47 – 6.42
2 years	6.60 – 6.55
3 years	6.80 – 6.75

Analysis
The company could meet its requirements by arranging three swaps, each of $10 million, with terms of one year, two years and three years respectively.

Swap	Company receives	Company pays
1 year	6.42%	12-month LIBOR
2 years	6.55%	12-month LIBOR
3 years	6.75%	12-month LIBOR

However, a swaps bank also could agree to offer a single amortizing swap instead of three separate swaps. The amortizing swap would combine the three separate annual rates of the individual swaps into a single rate for the full three-year term of the amortizing swap. There would be a single fixed rate receivable by the company, on notional principal of $30 million in Year 1, $20 million in Year 2 and $10 million in Year 3.

If the company wanted to match payments so that the swap receipts were exactly the same as the payments on the loan, the swaps bank would adjust the floating-rate swap payments accordingly.

LIBOR-in-Arrears Swaps

In a LIBOR-in-arrears swap, the floating rate for each interest period is set at the *end* of the period, and not, as with conventional swaps, at the start of each period. Settlement then takes place within two days of the reset/fixing date. This means that the parties to the swap do not know the floating-rate payment payable or receivable until the interest period has ended.

Example
Two parties agree to a swap on a notional principal of £10 million, with six-monthly fixing date. Alpha agrees to pay 6.8% fixed and receive LIBOR. One interest period runs from 7 June to 6 December. On 7 June LIBOR is 7%. On 6 December LIBOR is 6%.

Analysis
In a conventional swap, the floating rate payment by Beta for the six-month period 7 June to 6 December would be at 7%. Because Alpha is paying 6.8%, there would be a net payment in December from Beta to Alpha of 0.2% per annum, or £10,000 (£10 million x 0.2% x 6/12).

In a LIBOR-in-arrears swap, Beta would pay a variable rate of 6% for the six-month period, the LIBOR rate as at the end of the period. Alpha is paying 6.8%, so there would be a net payment from Alpha to Beta for the six-month period of 0.8% per annum or £40,000 (£10 million x 0.8% x 6/12). This would be payable on 8 December, two days after the fixing date of 6 December.

LIBOR-in-arrears swaps leave each counterparty exposed to the risk of an adverse movement in LIBOR during the interest-rate period. The variable-rate payer is at risk from a rise in LIBOR, and the receiver of variable rate is at risk from a fall in LIBOR.

As a result a company might try to arrange a LIBOR-in-arrears swap when it has a view about the likely direction of future movements in the LIBOR rate. If LIBOR is expected to fall, a variable-rate payer should prefer a LIBOR-in-arrears swap to a conventional swap.

Note: The fixed rate quoted in a LIBOR-in-arrears swap will differ from the conventional swap fixed rate. When the yield curve is upward-sloping, and long-term interest rates are higher than short-term rates, the

LIBOR-in-arrears fixed rates will be higher than comparable conventional swap fixed rates.

Conclusion

Other types of interest-rate swaps exist, and in an active and liquid market, new variations will continue to be developed to meet the requirements of particular customers.

Valuation of Swaps

An interest-rate swap is a contractual agreement between two parties to exchange a stream of interest payments on clearly defined terms. If interest rates are such that one party can expect to be a net receiver of interest payments, i.e. to receive more in interest than that party pays, the swap will have a positive money value for that party. Similarly, if the other party can expect to be a net payer of interest, the swap will have a negative value for the first party. The positive value of the swap for one party should, in principle, equal the negative value of the swap for the counterparty.

Example
Alpha and Omega Bank have a swap agreement that has a further four years to the end of its term. Alpha pays a fixed rate of 7% and receives LIBOR. Since the swap was arranged some time ago, fixed interest rates have fallen, and 5% would now be an appropriate fixed rate for a four-year swap. LIBOR is currently 4.5%.

Analysis
Omega Bank is receiving fixed interest at 7% and paying LIBOR, currently 4.5%. If the relevant market rates of interest remain around 5% for the next four years, Alpha will be committed to regular net payments to Omega Bank and Omega Bank can expect to receive regular net payments. The swap has a positive value for the bank, and a negative value for alpha. If interest rates, and expectations of interest-rate levels for the future, *change*, the value of the swap to both parties also will change.

Why Value Swaps?

There are several reasons for assessing the current value of swaps:

- Measuring profitability.
- Arranging non-par value swaps.
- Terminating a swap before maturity. If one party to a swap asks the other to terminate the swap before the end of its term, the compensation payable should be more than sufficient to cover the value of the swap at the date of its early termination.
- Assigning the swap to another party. One party to a swap may wish to assign its rights and obligations under the terms of the swap to a third party. In other words, one party might wish to sell its rights to someone else. The cash payment on assigning (selling) the swap will be the value of the swap that is agreed between the seller and the buyer.

Termination and assignment are explained further in Chapter 10.

Measuring Profitability
Banks that specialize in swaps have to monitor their swaps positions continually, and measure the profits or losses they are making. They do this by marking the value of their swaps to a current market value. Any rise or fall in the value of a swap position since the previous valuation is reported as a profit or loss.

Swaps Banks: Measuring Profits

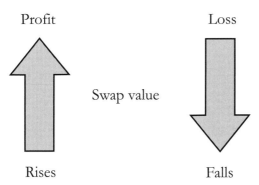

Arranging Non-Par Value Swaps

Some non-generic swaps include special features that modify its value, or could be deliberately priced at off-market rates to suit the requirements of one of the swap counterparties. In such cases, the swap will provide for an exchange of payments whereby one party is more likely than the other to be a net payer of interest, and the other party is more likely to be a net receiver of interest. These are non-par swaps, so called because they have a positive value to one party and a negative value to the other. When a swap is non-par at the time it is negotiated, one party will agree to compensate the other in some way, perhaps by paying an up-front fee to cover the value of the swap.

Valuing an Interest-Rate Swap

The value of a swap is measured by assessing the present value of the expected future interest receipts and future interest payments in the swap, using discounting arithmetic.

- The value of a coupon swap to the receiver of fixed interest is as follows:

Value of a Swap to the Receiver of Fixed Interest

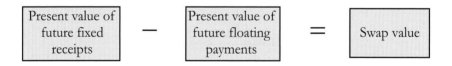

- Similarly, the value of a coupon swap to the payer of fixed interest is as follows:

Value of a Swap to the Payer of Fixed Interest

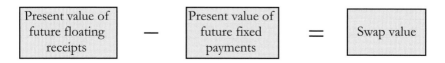

A *generic swap* has a zero value at the start of its term because the present value of expected future receipts equals the present value of expected future payments to both parties.

Value of a Generic Swap when Originally Transacted

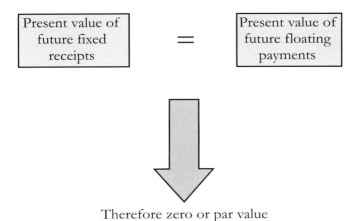

Therefore zero or par value

The mathematics of swap valuations can be fairly complex, but some simple examples will be used to explain the basic principles of valuation. Three issues to consider are:

- What interest rate should be used to discount expected future swap payments to a present value?
- How are fixed payments/receipts valued?
- How are floating-rate payments/receipts valued?

The Discount Rate
Selecting a suitable discount rate (interest rate) for the valuation of swaps is a fairly complex issue, although *zero coupon swap rates* are explained in the Appendix to this book. The simplifying assumption that will be used in this chapter for valuation purposes, is that future interest payments over the remaining term of the swap can be discounted at an appropriate swap rate, without explaining how this rate is obtained.

Valuation of Fixed Payments
The present value of future fixed payments in a swap is calculated by

discounting the future payments to a present value, using the current swap rate as the discounting rate.

A formula for calculating this present value is:

$$\text{Value of fixed payments} = P\left[\frac{1 - \left(1 + \frac{r}{100f}\right)^{-n}}{\frac{r}{100f}}\right]$$

Where:

- P is the amount of each fixed payment (annual or six-monthly, etc.)
- r is the swap rate for discounting (7% = 7, 6.25% = 6.25 etc.)
- f is the number of fixed payments each year, e.g. f = 2 when payments are six-monthly.
- n is the number of payments remaining before the end of the term of the swap.

Example
A generic coupon swap is arranged between a company and a bank in which the company receives interest at 8% per annum on notional principal of £10 million. The term of the swap is three years. Fixed payments are annual.

Analysis
Using 8% as the discount rate for the fixed payments in each year of the swap, the present value of the future fixed swap payments, at the start of the swap's term, is:

$$£800,000 \left[\frac{1 - (1.08)^{-3}}{0.08}\right]$$

$$= £800,000 \, (2.5771)$$
$$= £2,061,680$$

Valuation of Floating-Rate Payments
The value of floating-rate payments cannot be measured in the same way as the fixed payments, by discounting a future income stream, because

the amount of these future floating payments is uncertain. The size of each payment depends on how the floating rate index, e.g. LIBOR, fluctuates over time.

For coupon swaps, however, a useful starting point for the valuation of the floating-rate payments is that a generic swap has a zero value at the start of its term. This means that the present value of future floating-rate payments based on the agreed index, e.g. six-month LIBOR, must be the same as the present value of the fixed payments over the term of the swap, discounted at the appropriate current swap rate.

Example
Let's return to the example of the generic swap above. At the start of the term of the swap, the present value of the future fixed payments is £2,061,680.

Because it is a generic swap, the present value of the expected future floating-rate payments must be the same.

Another approach to floating-rate payments is to measure their value in terms of the notional principal amount in the swap. It could be assumed that the payer of the floating-rate interest borrows the notional principal, on which interest is then payable, and repays it at the end of the swap's term. The present value of the interest payments would be the difference between the notional principal and the present value of the notional principal at the end of the swap's term. This present value can be calculated as:

$$NP \times \frac{1}{\left(1 + \frac{r}{100}\right)^n}$$

Where:

- NP is the notional principal
- r is the swap rate for discounting, as an annual rate (8% = 8, etc)
- n is the number of years to the end of the swap's term

Example
Let's return again to the previous example of the generic swap with a three-year term, in which a company receives fixed interest at 8% and pays LIBOR, on notional principal of £10 million.

Analysis
Using 8% as the discount rate for the cash flows in each year of the swap, the present value of the future floating-rate payments, as at the start of the swap's term, is:

$$£10,000,000 - \left[£10,000,000 \times \frac{1}{(1.08)^3}\right]$$
$$= £10,000,000 - £7,938,320$$
$$= £2,061,680$$

If you refer back to the valuation of the fixed payments in this swap, you will see that the fixed payments and floating payments have the same present value, as at the start of the swap's term. This, remember, is a feature of generic swaps at the start of their term.

Valuation of Non-Par Swaps
Generic swaps will acquire a value over time when interest rates change. The same principles of valuation are applied to estimate the current value of non-par swaps.

Example
Let's return again to the previous example of the generic three-year swap, for which the fixed rate payments are 8% and the notional principal is £10 million. Suppose that after one year, interest rates have fallen and an appropriate market rate for a two-year swap is now 6.5%.

Analysis
The fall in interest rates benefits the receiver of the fixed rate in the swap because the receiver of the fixed rate is now receiving fixed payments at above the current market rate. The floating rate will have fallen too, and the receiver of the fixed rate, in this example the

company, will be receiving more in fixed interest under the swap than it pays in floating-rate interest to the swaps bank.

The value of the future fixed receipts is now:

$$£800,000 \left[\frac{1 - (1.065)^{-2}}{0.065} \right]$$
$$= £800,000 \,(1.820626)$$
$$= £1,456,501$$

The present value of the future floating-rate payments can be based on the assumption that it is the same as the present value of fixed-rate payments on a new generic two-year swap (two years because this is the remaining term of the swap), discounted at the current swap rate.

Assuming that the current swap rate is 6.5% for each of the two remaining years of the swap, the present value of the future floating-rate payments will be:

$$£650,000 \left[\frac{1 - (1.065)^{-2}}{0.065} \right]$$
$$= £650,000 \,(1.820626)$$
$$= £1,183,407$$

Therefore the value of the swap is:

	£
Present value of fixed payments	1,456,501
Present value of floating payments	1,183,407
Difference: value to receiver of fixed payments	273,094

The present value of the fixed payments is higher. The swap therefore has a positive value of £273,094 to the receiver of the fixed payments at the end of its first year, and a negative value of the same amount to the payer of the fixed interest.

The alternative approach to the valuation of the floating-rate payments is:

$$£10,000,000 - \left[\frac{£10,000,000 \times 1}{(1.065)^2}\right]$$
$$= £10,000,000 - £8,816,593$$
$$= £1,183,407$$

This is the same figure as calculated by the other method.

Exercise
Try to find your own solution to this problem.

A coupon swap has three years remaining to maturity. Fixed interest payments are six-monthly, at 4% (semi-annual basis) on the notional principal of $30 million. (You may assume that fixed payments are 2% of $30 million each six months.) Floating-rate payments are at six-month dollar LIBOR.

The current swap rate for a three-year swap is 5% per annum sab. You may assume that this is the appropriate rate to use for discounting the future cash flows under the swap.

What is the current value of the swap?

Solution
Fixed payments
The value of the fixed payments is the present value of six six-monthly payments of $600,000 (2% of $30 million) over the next three years, discounted at the current swap rate of 5% per annum semi-annual basis. The annual rate is 5% but there are two interest payments each year. The value of f in the formula therefore is 2.

$$\$600,000 \left[\frac{1 - \left(1 + \frac{5}{200}\right)^{-6}}{\frac{5}{200}}\right]$$

$= \$600,000 \ (0.137703/0.025)$
$= \$600,000 \ (5.508125)$
$= \$3,304,875$

Floating payments

The value of the floating payments is the same as the present value of the fixed payments in a generic swap arranged now, i.e. with a term of three years and an interest rate of 5% sab on notional principal of $30 million. The six-monthly fixed swap payments would be $750,000 (6/12 x 5% x $30 million).

The value is:

$$\$750{,}000 \left[\frac{1 - \left(1 + \frac{5}{200}\right)^{-6}}{\frac{5}{200}} \right]$$

= $750,000 (5.508125)
= $4,131,094.

Value of the swap

The value of the swap is:

	$
Present value of fixed payments	3,304,875
Present value of floating payments	4,131,094
Difference: value to payer of fixed payments	826,219

The value of the swap is $826,219. The value of the floating payments exceeds the value of the fixed payments. The swap therefore has a positive value to the payer of the fixed payments, and an equal negative value to the receiver of the fixed payments.

Conclusion

The explanations and illustrations in this chapter have been simplified for the sake of clarity. The key points to note, however, are that:

- the value of a swap is the difference between the present value of the expected future receipts and the present value of the expected future payments, to the end of the term of the swap

- a generic swap has a zero value (par value) at the beginning of its term
- swaps change in value with changes in market interest rates
- the increase in the value of a swap to one party should be matched by an equal fall in the value of the swap to the other party
- swaps banks report profits and losses on their swaps positions as the value of these positions changes, i.e. as the value of their swaps changes.

Administration of Swaps

The previous chapters have described what swaps are and why they are used. This chapter looks at the who, when and how; in other words, who uses swaps, when is the best time to arrange them and how they are arranged and administered.

Who Uses Swaps?

The minimum swap is normally for a principal amount of $5 million, so most often swaps are used by only medium-sized or large companies and organizations.

Most swaps trading is between banks. Some banks trade in swaps for profit while others use swaps to match their funding cash flows. For example, if a bank is funding fixed-rate loans to customers with variable-rate borrowings, it can swap from variable rate into fixed rate, and match interest receivable from its customers with the fixed-rate swap payments. Swaps also are used by:

- other financial institutions – savings and loan funds, insurance companies, building societies, etc.
- supranational organizations such as the World Bank and European Investment Bank
- governments and government agencies
- companies, particularly multinational and international companies.

When to Swap

A decision to arrange a swap is likely to be prompted by a change, either in market rates of interest or in a company's view about future interest rate movements.

A change in market rates of interest, either fixed or variable, could open a temporary window of opportunity for arranging a swap at a favorable net rate of interest. Such opportunities are likely to be short-lived, and would have to be exploited quickly.

A change in a company's view about a future movement in interest rates could persuade a company to negotiate a swap, but it would not be under the same time pressure to make the arrangement. If the company expects interest rates to rise, it might seek to swap its variable-rate loan payments into fixed-rate payments. If it expects interest rates to fall, it might seek to swap its fixed-rate obligations into variable-rate payments.

How to Arrange Swaps

A company or bank may be considering a swap because it wants to raise funds at a fixed interest rate but cannot do so in the primary market. It will approach one of its relationship banks or perhaps another bank that specializes in swaps. Alternatively, a bank specializing in swaps might approach a company, first suggesting that a swap arrangement could be beneficial and then offering to set up one. A bank might also act as a *broker* for a company, identifying another banking counterparty whose swap pricing is more competitive than its own.

The Primary Market: Banks

The primary market for swaps refers to the transaction of initial swap agreements. Banks play an intermediary role as:

- *Arrangers*, i.e. acting as broker/agent for two clients who transact a swap directly between each other.
- *Matched book dealers*, i.e. acting as principal in two or more matching swaps, transacted at about the same time and for about the same amount of notional principal, each with a different counterparty. For example, a bank might transact two matching swaps, one in which it is a payer of fixed interest on $20 million and the second with a different counterparty in which it is a receiver of fixed interest on $20 million.
- *Market makers in swaps*. Some banks are willing to make a market in swaps and act as principal in swap transactions without necessarily arranging matching swaps with other parties. Most market makers nevertheless aim to run a matched book in swaps, but will accept and manage the risk from temporarily unmatched positions. Market makers set swap rates in the market.

Example

Suppose you are a swaps trader. Another bank calls to ask your price in five-year dollar-interest rate swaps. The market is 60/50 over the Treasury bond yield, but you think rates and swap spreads are going to increase.

Analysis

Suppose you quote 65/55. Your bid of 55, where you pay the fixed rate, is better than the market rate of 50. If the other bank wants to be the receiver of the fixed rate, it will deal with you. If it wants to be a payer of the fixed rate, it will find your quote of 65 too expensive.

Suppose you quoted 55/45 instead. Your offer of 55, where you receive the fixed rate, is cheaper than the market price of 60. If the other bank wants to be a payer of the fixed rate, it will deal with you.

The principle involved in market making is to enhance the price on the side of the market where you want to deal and simultaneously quote a less attractive price than the rest of the market on the side where you do not want to deal.

Broking Firms

There are some organizations that act as broker in swap arrangements, finding the most suitable swaps bank for a client. A broker should have total knowledge of the swaps market, and be able to protect the anonymity of clients until a match for their position is found. For all but the largest corporate clients, a broker also should be able to find a better rate than the company could find. A commission is charged for brokerage services, but only on conclusion of the swap transaction for the customer. Brokers work on the principle of no transaction, no fee.

Brokerage fees are paid up front and typically are in the region of one basis point (0.01%) of the notional principal. A broker will give indicative swap rates that it can obtain, and display these on price information screens, but brokers do not act as a counterparty in a swap.

The indicative rates are for standard transactions and will differ for example when:

- a client wants a swap to match its own specific payment dates
- the transaction is either very large or small
- there is a significant difference in the credit quality of the counterparties in the swap.

A brokered deal would be arranged with the broker finding two parties wishing to swap in opposite directions, who agree in principle to swap terms outlined by the broker. (The rate is agreed subject to credit.) The broker gives the name of the swap counterparty to each client, who can then carry out a credit check. If the credit is acceptable, the broker then acts as a go-between for the arrangement, negotiating in particular on the price (swap rate). If agreement is reached, the swap is transacted directly between the broker's two clients.

The Negotiating Process

The market in interest-rate swaps is an over-the-counter market, although LIFFE, the London futures exchange, trades some swap futures contracts. Negotiations are conducted mostly by telephone, although prices are disseminated through screen-based information systems.

The key financial details of a swap are agreed verbally between the parties. After verbal agreement, these details are confirmed, usually within 24 hours, by an exchange of messages.

The contract documentation is then drawn up and signed. A legal contract for a swap transaction generally is assumed to exist when the verbal agreement is reached, rather than when the confirmations are exchanged or the contract documentation is signed.

In a coupon swap, the most important negotiating detail is the rate, i.e. the fixed-rate payable/receivable. When a swap is quoted in terms of a spread above a benchmark yield, for example as a number of basis points over the Treasury bond yield, the parties will first of all reach agreement on the size of the spread, rather than the outright fixed rate, subject to credit.

Negotiations will be halted temporarily, so that each party can carry out a credit check on the other. A credit check involves confirming that:

- the credit limit for dealing with the other party is large enough, and
- there is enough room under existing credit limits to arrange the swap.

Subject to credit clearance, the parties will contact each other again, and agree the fixed rate. The previously agreed spread over the Treasury's yield is added to current yield, to determine the fixed all-in interest rate for the swap.

The negotiating process is illustrated in the flowchart opposite.

Swap Negotiating Process

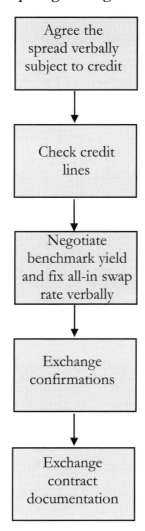

Terminology

It is important that in negotiating a swap with a bank, the customer should understand the terminology used correctly. Each party will look at the arrangement from its own viewpoint, that will be the opposite viewpoint of the counterparty, and confusion could arise. Specifying clearly the desired movement of interest payments should prevent ambiguity. For example, the customer should state whether it wishes to receive the fixed and pay the floating (variable rate), or pay the fixed and receive the variable.

Contract Terms

A swap is a contract formalized by a legal agreement, signed by both parties. Terms and conditions in a swap agreement include:

- *Payments.* The interest-rate basis for calculating the swap payments, the notional principal and the timing of payments must all be specified.
- *Event of default.* It is necessary to set out the conditions whereby a party to the agreement would be considered in default. An event of default will give the injured counterparty grounds for taking action.
- *Termination.* A swap is a binding contract on both parties, but conditions under which a swap can be terminated are specified.

Swap trading used to be severely restricted by the complexities of the contract documentation. To overcome the delays and costs of agreeing swaps contracts, the parties to a swap now use standard documentation wherever possible. Standardization is promoted through market associations, notably the International Swaps and Derivatives Association (ISDA) and the British Bankers' Association.

Standard terms and conditions for interest-rate swaps have been established by ISDA, initially in New York but now throughout the world. In the UK standard terms and conditions were established in 1985 for *interbank* swaps by the British Bankers' Association Interest Rate Swaps standard terms (BBAIRS).

ISDA Documentation
ISDA provides comprehensive and standardized swaps documentation. A standard master swap agreement, when completed by two parties, becomes a signed contract, covering the terms of all swaps subsequently

transacted between them. The details of each new swap are added to the master contract as an appendix. Each time a new swap is added, a new contract is created to encompass all the swap transactions still outstanding between the parties, a process called *novation*. ISDA documentation is used widely for long-term swaps between counterparties that transact swap deals regularly, e.g. two banks.

If a company transacts swaps regularly with a particular bank, it might seek to arrange a Master Swaps Agreement based on ISDA documentation, removing the necessity for extensive documentation for each individual swap agreement.

Closing Out a Swap

On occasion a company might want to close out a swap arrangement before it reaches the end of its term. The reason could be that the company wants to revert back from floating rate to fixed rate, or from fixed-rate to floating-rate payments. Alternatively, the swap could have been arranged for an underlying loan that has now been repaid, or an underlying investment that is no longer held.

Closing out a swap can be done in one of the following ways:

- termination
- assignment (buyout)
- reversal.

Termination
A party to a swap, usually the customer, can ask the counterparty, usually the swaps bank, for the agreement to be terminated. The bank, if it agrees, might charge a negotiable termination fee to cover its administration costs. In addition, there will be a one-off payment from one party to the other, based on the current value of the swap (see Chapter 9). If the swap has a positive value for the bank, i.e. if payment is due from the customer to the bank, the bank will seek payment in full. If, however, interest rates have moved so that a payment is due on

termination from the bank to the customer, the bank is likely to try to negotiate a reduced payment.

Example
A company has a swap on notional principal of $20 million that has three more years to run. Swap payments are exchanged once a year, with the company paying 12-month LIBOR and receiving 6.40% per annum fixed. The company wishes to terminate the swap and approaches the counterparty, a swaps bank. 12-month LIBOR is currently 7.40% per annum.

Analysis
If 12-month LIBOR remained 7.40% for the next three years, the company would make annual net swap payments of 1% per annum (7.40-6.40%) on notional principal of $20 million. This would amount to $200,000 each year for three years. The swap would be terminated with the company making a payment to the swaps bank of the present value equivalent of these payments, and possibly in addition a termination fee.

If interest rates had moved in the company's favor, it might not wish to terminate the swap unless it could obtain a compensation payment from the swaps bank, although this can be difficult to negotiate.

Exercise
Try you own solution to this problem.

A company has transacted a swap on a notional principal of £10 million to pay a fixed rate of 8% for a period of seven years and receive six-month LIBOR. It now wants to terminate the arrangement three years from maturity when the three-year fixed swap rate is 5.60-5.50%. What is the amount of the settlement payment to terminate the swap, before discounting to a present value?

Solution
The settlement for termination should compensate the counterparty (the swaps bank) for the difference between the fixed rate in the swap and

the current market rate (fixed) for the term to maturity of the swap, in this example three years. The amount of compensation before discounting will be the 2.5% differential in interest rates between the fixed rate paid on the swap and the fixed rate that the swaps bank would now expect to receive (8% -5.50%). On £10 million this will be £125,000 every six months (1.25% per half year) for the next three years. A discount rate will be applied to calculate the present value of these payments and so determinate the actual amount payable.

Assignment (Buyout)
A swap position can be closed by paying another bank to take over as the swap counterparty. Suppose, for example, that Delta has a swap agreement with Omega Bank. Delta pays a fixed rate of 5% and receives six-month LIBOR, currently 6.5% per annum. Interest exchanges currently are settled by a net payment from the bank to Delta. Delta now wishes to close its swap position, but Omega Bank is unwilling to pay a termination settlement large enough to satisfy Delta. The company therefore approaches another bank, Epsilon Bank, that agrees to a buy-out of Delta's swap position and quotes a buy-out price it is willing to pay. Delta agrees, but before a buy-out can be transacted Omega Bank must agree to the replacement of Delta by Epsilon Bank as counterparty to the swap.

Reversal
A swap position can be closed out by arranging a second and opposite swap that reverses the original swap. For example, suppose that a company has a swap on notional principal of $20 million that has three years left to the end of its term, in which the company pays a fixed rate and receives six-month LIBOR. It could close its position by arranging a second swap with a three-year term and on the same amount of notional principal, in which it pays six-month LIBOR and receives a fixed rate. There will be two swaps in place until the final maturity, and each swap has to be administered. The fixed rate in each swap is most unlikely to be the same, and there will be a regular net receipt or net payment under the swap agreement for each six-monthly exchange of payments up to the end to the term of both swaps.

Example

A company has a swap agreement with notional principal of $20 million. It pays a fixed rate of 6% and receives six-month LIBOR. The swap has two years left to maturity. The company wishes to close its position now, and a swap bank has quoted prices of 5.95-5.85% for a two-year swap.

Analysis

To close the position by reversal, the company would arrange a second swap. This would be for the same amount of notional principal and a two-year term. The company would pay six-month LIBOR and receive fixed 5.85%.

Its overall position on reversal will be:

		%
Original swap:	Pay	- 10.00
	Receive	+ LIBOR
Reversing swap	Pay	- LIBOR
	Receive	+ 5.85
Net position	Pay	- 0.15

There will be a net payment every six months until the end of the term of the swaps, from the company to the swaps bank. Each payment will be about $15,000 ($20 million x 6/12 x 0.15%).

Swaps and Financial Risk

Swaps can be used to hedge exposures to financial risk.

- *Interest rate swaps* can be used to hedge exposures to the risk of losses from changes in interest rates.
- *Currency swaps* can be used to hedge exposures to the risk of losses from changes in exchange rates.

On the other hand, swaps also can create exposures to financial risk. Interest rate swaps in a single currency give rise to both

- credit risk and
- possibly interest-rate risk.

Swaps and Credit Risk

When two parties enter a swap transaction, they take on the risk that the counterparty might default on its obligations, and fail to make a payment when it falls due.

The size of the credit risk will depend on the length of the remaining term of the swap, and on interest rates. Suppose, for example, that in a swap with four more years remaining to the end of its term, a bank is a payer of fixed interest at 5.5% against receipt of floating rate at LIBOR, on notional principal of $20 million. Suppose also that LIBOR is now 6.5%.

If the other party were to default on its swaps obligations, the bank would lose the net payments due to it under the terms of the swap. Currently, these favor the bank by 1%, or $200,000 per annum. If interest rates did not change again during the remaining life of the swap, the bank's credit risk would be $800,000, $200,000 per annum for each of the remaining four years. If interest rates were to rise, the credit risk would be even higher because the net swap payments due from the counterparty would then be greater than $200,000 per annum.

It is important to recognize the nature of the credit risk in an interest-rate swap. Because no principal is exchanged, the credit risk is restricted to the possibility that the other party will stop exchanging interest payments.

- If an interest rate swap is used to speculate on movements in market rates of interest, default by one party will deprive the other of the opportunity for speculative profits.
- If the swap is being used to hedge an interest-rate exposure, default by the other party will leave the exposure unhedged. An actual cost will then be suffered if, as a consequence, higher interest costs were to be incurred.

Example
A company has arranged a coupon swap in which it receives fixed interest at 6%. This hedges an exposure to fixed payments on a bond issue by the company, for which the coupon rate is also 6%. If the counterparty in the swap (the payer of fixed interest) subsequently defaults, and the market rate of interest has now fallen, for example to 4%, the hedge for the exposure will be lost. Because interest rates have fallen by 2% since the start of the swap, the company will incur higher interest costs of 2% per annum. If the swap counterparty had not defaulted, the company would have been a payer of LIBOR, now around 4%. Because of the default, the company is paying the fixed rate in the bonds, that is 6%.

Quantifying the Credit Risk

The amount of the credit risk in a coupon swap is the current value of the swap. In other words, if the swap has a positive value, default by the other party would wipe out this value.

Example
Theta Bank arranged a five-year generic swap with Alpha. Notional principal was $100 million. Theta Bank paid 5% fixed (annually) and received six-month LIBOR.

After two years, when the swap's term still has three years to run, Alpha defaulted. For a three-year swap on similar terms to the old swap, suppose the fixed rate would be 6.5%, and that this is the appropriate rate for discounting in order to value the remaining swap payments in each future year.

Analysis
The present value of the remaining fixed payments on the existing swap is:

$$5\% \text{ of } \$100 \text{ million} \times \left[\frac{1-(1.065)^{-3}}{0.065}\right]$$

$= \$5 \text{ million } (2.6485)$
$= \$13.243 \text{ million}$

The present value of the remaining floating-rate payments to maturity is equal to the present value of the fixed payments (at 6.5%) in a new generic three-year swap.

$$6.5\% \text{ of } \$100 \text{ million} \times \left[\frac{1-(1.065)^{-3}}{0.065}\right]$$

$= \$650,000 \ (2.6485)$
$= \$17,215 \text{ million}$

The value of the swap to Theta Bank, that pays the fixed interest and receives the floating, is therefore $3.972 million ($17.215 million − $13.243 million). When Alpha defaults, this value is lost. As a consequence Theta Bank will incur a loss of $3.972 million.

The swaps market is very credit-sensitive. Many organizations refuse to enter into swap transactions with counterparties whose credit status is below a certain level.

Swaps and Interest-Rate Risk

When a bank or other company enters a swap agreement it commits itself contractually to exchanging a series of interest-rate payments into the future. Market rates of interest could move up or down, so that in retrospect it would have been better for one of the parties to have avoided the swap altogether. As a result of the changes in market interest rates, one party to the swap will benefit and the other will suffer a loss.

Example
Two banks, Alpha and Zeta, arrange a swap in which Alpha pays 6% fixed and receives six-month LIBOR, on notional principal of $100 million.

The payments made by one bank to the other over the term of the swap will depend on the difference between six-month LIBOR and the fixed 6% rate, i.e. on the size and direction of changes in six-month LIBOR.

The graph over the page illustrates how changes in LIBOR over the period would work to the benefit of one bank at the expense of the other.

Swaps and Interest-Rate Risk

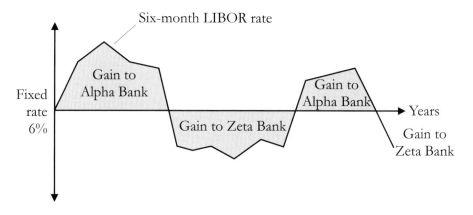

Suppose, for example, that a company with variable-rate borrowings locks into fixed-rate payments using an interest-rate swap. The company must accept that if subsequently market-interest rates fall, it will end up paying more than it would have done if it had opted to stay with variable-rate interest payments. In other words, it will incur higher costs because it will be a net payer of interest in the swap.

These net swap payments could be regarded as part of the company's interest cost, adding to the overall interest charge. As extra payments, they are expenditures or losses to be written off to the company's profit and loss account.

Example
Some years ago, a Dallas oil rig operator arranged a three-year interest rate swap for $85 million, swapping from variable-rate payments on the debt to become a fixed-rate payer in the swap at about 7.5%. Subsequently it was reported that the company expected interest rates to rise, and therefore believed that the swap would secure a low fixed-rate interest cost over the three-year period. In the event, interest rates fell, and the company ended up paying well over $5 million more with the swap than it would have paid without it.

Basis Risk and Maturity Risk

Swaps can expose an organization to basis risk and maturity risk that are both aspects of interest-rate risk. Basis risk arises from the possibility of a change in the size of the difference between one short-term (money market) rate of interest and another. Maturity risk occurs when the timing of swap payments and the swap's maturity do not coincide exactly with the underlying payments/loans for which the swap provides a hedge.

Basis risk arises with basis swaps. Suppose, for example, that one party in a swap pays three-month LIBOR and receives six-month LIBOR. If the difference between three-month and six-month LIBOR changes, one party will profit and the other will lose.

Basis risk also can occur when a company establishes a commercial paper program, issuing short-dated commercial paper at regular intervals, and uses a swap to convert the variable-rate payments, the rate payable on each successive issue of CP, into a fixed rate. The swap might be a coupon swap in which the company pays a fixed rate and receives six-month LIBOR.

- Basis risk will occur because the interest-rate swap has LIBOR as the floating-rate benchmark, but the company will be paying a different rate on its commercial paper. Changes in the difference between LIBOR and the CP rate will alter the company's overall interest costs.
- Maturity risk also would occur if the payment dates for the swap differed from the issue/redemption dates for the CP. Changes in interest rates between the differing maturity dates also would affect the company's overall cost of funding.

Accounting for Profits or Losses on Interest-Rate Swaps

Banks that trade in swaps report profits or losses on their swaps activities by marking-to-market the value of their swaps positions. Marking-to-market involves the anticipated future stream of interest payments being converted into a current market value. An increase in value represents a profit, and a fall in value results in a loss. Profits or losses on swaps positions will occur, using a mark-to-market approach, whenever interest rates change.

For example, suppose that a bank arranges a swap with an estimated zero net value in which it pays fixed interest at 6% and receives LIBOR.

- If market interest rates rise, the swap will acquire a positive value for the bank that would now be paying a fixed rate in the swap that is below the current market rate of interest, but receiving the current LIBOR rate. The increase in the swap's value would be reported as a profit.
- If market interest rates fall, the swap will lose value for the bank and any fall in value will be reported as a loss.

The method of valuing swaps is explained in Chapter 9.

Non-bank corporates could report profits or losses on their swaps positions by marking-to-market in the same way. Alternatively, where the swap has been arranged to hedge an interest-rate exposure, the company simply might report the periodic swap payments or receipts as expenditure or income in its profit and loss account. For example, if a company borrows money at a variable rate and uses a swap to convert its net payments into a fixed rate, it might choose to account for the swap as synthetic fixed-rate debt, instead of accounting for the actual variable-rate payments and the swap payments/receipts as two separate items. The company's published accounts would be expected to provide information about the swap in a note.

There has been some disagreement about how non-bank corporates should account for derivative instruments, including swaps. A problem with the hedge-accounting approach is that if the underlying exposure disappears, or if the hedge is found to be inappropriate, the company might then have to report a large gain or loss on its swap position.

The financial accounting regulation FAS 115, introduced in 1994, requires that securities, including derivatives, be categorized as:

- held to maturity
- available for sale, or
- held for trading.

Any securities falling into the second or third of these categories should be marked-to-market, and any changes in their value reported as gains or losses.

Regulation and Financial Risk

The large financial risks that can arise with derivatives raise questions about the ability of banks to sustain any losses that might arise from their derivative positions. Guidelines have been issued by banking regulators and securities regulators as to how risks should be monitored and controled.

The Bank for International Settlements, for example, has issued guidelines that state:

- the board of directors of banks should be informed regularly about the risk exposures of their bank
- banks dealing in foreign exchange, derivatives and other traded instruments should be able to mark their positions to market at least daily (and preferably in real time)
- banks also should pay close attention to the credit risk they incur from selling over-the-counter derivative products such as swaps.

Banks have argued that their total exposure to risk from swaps is much less than the nominal amount of principal on their current swap transactions. For example, if a bank has a swaps book of $1 billion in notional principal, the potential exposure to losses from credit risk and interest rate risk will be much less than this amount. Even so, risk exposures in the banking industry are very large.

Appendix: Zero Coupon Rates

Par and Non-Par Swaps

A par swap is a swap for which the fixed rate payable/receivable is equal to the current market rate. To transact a generic swap, for example, a swaps bank will pay or receive its current quoted par swap rate in exchange for LIBOR flat. In swaps terminology, coupon is a term commonly used to mean a par swap.

In practise, however, many swaps are not par swaps. For example, a swap might be arranged so that the fixed-interest payment matches exactly the fixed-interest payments on an underlying bond issue, where the bond does not have a par value.

Suppose for example that an investment company holds a quantity of 4% bonds that have a current market price of just 95.00, and it wants to swap its fixed rate of income for a floating rate. The bond does not have a par value, i.e. its price is not exactly 100, and a generic swap transaction would not be feasible. A swaps bank might be willing to arrange a swap with the investment company whereby it receives fixed payments at 4% and in exchange pays a floating rate of LIBOR minus a number of basis points. If the bond had been valued above par, the bank would have paid LIBOR plus a number of basis points.

However, the problem is to decide what the number of basis points above or below LIBOR should be.

To understand the principles of setting the rate for a non-par swap, it is necessary to know something about the zero coupon swap rate, that is also known more academically as the spot rate.

Terminology
Spot   =   Zero Coupon
Coupon   =   Par Swap

When the yield curve is normal and upward-sloping, the zero coupon swap rate (spot) is a few basis points higher than the coupon rate (par swap rate).

Obtaining a Zero Coupon Rate

A zero coupon instrument, such as a zero coupon bond, is one on which there is no payment to the holder until maturity. The holder receives a single payment at maturity. A zero coupon bond, for example, might be issued at a price below par and redeemed at par. No interest would be paid until redemption, and the interest to the bondholder would be represented by the difference between the issue price and the redemption price. Zero coupon money-market instruments include short-term inter-bank loans, Treasury bills and bank bills.

For swaps, there is usually a series of interest payments at regular intervals until the end of the term of the swap. However, it is possible to strip out each separate payment, and treat it as a stand-alone zero coupon instrument. (Bond strips work on this principle.) An interest rate appropriate to each stand-alone payment, the zero coupon rate, then can be derived from current market (coupon) rates.

Example
A bond with an 8% coupon, paying interest annually, will mature in exactly three years' time. It is redeemable at par.

Analysis
The future payments on the bond, per 100 nominal value of bonds, will be:

Year	Amount
1	8
2	8
3	108

The market value of a bond is the present value of its future payments to maturity, interest and principal. To derive zero coupon rates, we can say that the value of the bond is the sum of the present values of three separate zero coupon instruments:

- a one-year zero coupon bond, paying 8 at the end of Year 1
- a two-year zero coupon bond, paying 8 at the end of Year 2
- a three-year zero coupon bond, paying 108 at the end of Year 3.

From Coupon Rates to Zero Coupon (Spot) Rates

We can now derive zero coupon rates for Years 1, 2 and 3 from the coupon rates on bonds with 1, 2 and 3 years to maturity. (To simplify the illustration, annual interest rate payments are assumed in this example.)

Example

Suppose that par swap rates (coupon rates) quoted in the swaps market are:

Maturity (years)	Coupon rate %	Interest frequency
1	8.00	Annual
2	8.49	Annual
3	8.73	Annual

Analysis

These rates indicate that:

- a one-year bond paying interest annually will have a par value of 100 if its coupon rate of interest is 8.00%
- a two-year bond paying interest annually will have a par value of 100 if its coupon rate of interest is 8.49%, i.e. if interest is payable annually at 8.49% on the nominal value of the bond

APPENDIX: ZERO COUPON RATES

- a three-year bond paying interest annually will have a par value of 100 if its coupon rate of interest is 8.73%.

Bond	Current value	Future payments		
		Year 1	Year 2	Year 3
1-year bond	100	108.00	-	-
2-year bond	100	8.49	108.49	-
3-year bond	100	8.73	8.73	108.73

Let us start by looking at the two-year bond. A two-year bond paying 8.49 at the end of Year 1 and 108.49 at the end of Year 2 has a par value of 100. We can analyze the payments on this bond as two separate zero coupon payments, on two separate zero coupon bonds, but with a combined market value of 100:

- one bond will pay 8.49 after one year
- the other bond will pay 108.49 after two years.

We know that the interest rate on a one-year bond is 8.00%. We can calculate the present value of a one-year zero coupon bond paying 8.49 after one year by discounting 8.49 at a one-year rate of 8.00%.

$$\frac{8.49}{(1.08)^1} = 7.6811$$

We know that a bond paying 8.49 after one year and 108.49 after two years has a par value of 100. So if a zero coupon bond paying 8.49 after one year has a value of 7.6811, it follows that the value of a two-year zero coupon bond paying 108.49 at the end of Year 2 has a value of (100 – 7.8611) 92.1389.

We now know the present value of a two-year zero coupon instrument, 92.1389, and the amount that it will pay at the end of Year 2, 108.49. Therefore we can calculate the annual interest rate for this zero coupon instrument using the following approach.

$$\frac{FV_n}{PV_o} = (1 + r)^n$$

Where:

- FV_n is the amount of the zero coupon payment at maturity, at the end of Year n
- PV_o is the present value of the zero coupon instrument
- r is the zero coupon annual interest rate for a maturity of n years (5% = 0.05, etc)
- n is the number of years to maturity of the zero coupon instrument.

In this example:

$$\frac{108.49}{92.1389} = (1 + r)^2$$

$$\frac{1.17746}{(1 + r)} = (1 + r)^2$$

$$(1 + r) = 1.0851$$

$$r = 0.0851, \text{ or } 8.51\%.$$

We have thus converted a two-year coupon rate of 8.49% for a par value bond or swap into a one-year zero coupon rate of 8.00% and a two-year zero coupon rate of 8.51%.

In a similar way, we can use the three-year coupon (par swap) rate of 8.73% to derive a three-year zero coupon rate, using the 8.00% zero coupon rate for one year and the 8.51% zero coupon rate for two years.

Year	Payment	Discount rate	Discount factor	Present value
1	8.73	8.00%	$1/(1.08)$	8.0833
2	8.73	8.51%	$1/(1.0851)^2$	7.4144
3	108.73	r	$1/(1 + r)^3$	84.5023
			Total par value	100.0000

The present value of the Year 3 zero coupon payment of 108.73 is simply the balancing figure, calculated by deducting the value of the Year 1 and Year 2 zero coupon payments from the par value of 100.

The three-year zero coupon rate is now calculated as follows:

$$\frac{108.73}{84.5023} = (1+r)^3$$
$$1.28671 = (1+r)^3$$
$$(1+r) = 1.0877$$
$$r = 0.0877, \text{ i.e. } 8.77\%.$$

Zero coupon rates can be calculated in a similar way for bonds and swaps with any other maturity, e.g. four years, five years, six years, ten years, twenty years, and so on.

Zero Coupon Swap Curve

Zero coupon swap rates can be calculated for each maturity to obtain a zero coupon swap curve. Zero coupon rates have been shown in the previous examples for instruments with annual coupon interest payments. In practise, semi-annual coupons also are common, but zero coupon rates can be calculated for these in much the same way as for annual coupons.

Information providers such as Bloomberg provide information screens that show:

- coupon rates for par swaps, and spot rates (zero coupon rates), and
- the zero coupon swap curve.

The following illustrates how coupon rates and spot rates (zero coupon rates) might be shown at a given date and in a particular currency.

Forward curve analysis

(Date)	FRQ	Coupon	Spot
1 wk		6.1875	6.1875
1 mo		6.1875	6.1875
2 mo		6.3750	6.3750
3 mo		6.6250	6.6250
4 mo		6.8125	6.8125
5 mo		7.0000	7.0000
6 mo		7.1875	7.1875
9 mo		7.5625	7.5625
1 yr		8.0000	8.0000
2 yrs	s	8.4900	8.5282
3 yrs	s	8.7300	8.7787
4 yrs	s	8.8000	8.8472
5 yrs	s	8.8900	8.9464
7 yrs	s	9.0200	9.0955
10 yrs	s	9.0600	9.1261

FRQ = frequency of interest payments, and s means semi-annual.

The numbers shown in this table can be represented graphically, in a zero coupon swap curve, as in the graph opposite.

APPENDIX: ZERO COUPON RATES

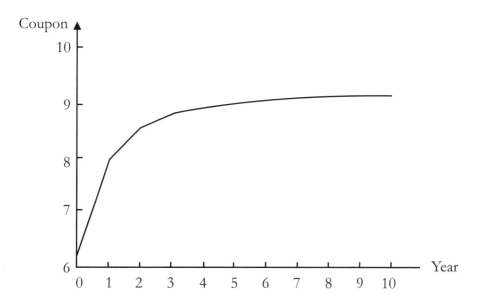

Zero Coupon Rates and Non-Par Swaps

The significance of zero coupon rates is that they can be used to value non-par instruments. For example, suppose that a bond with 7% coupon and paying interest annually has exactly three years to maturity, and a current market value of just 96.00. An investment company holding $10 million (nominal value) of the bonds wants to swap its fixed-interest receipts into floating rate. The zero coupon rates are:

Year	
1	8.00%
2	8.51%
3	8.77%

A swaps bank can use the zero coupon rates to compare the fixed annual payments it would receive under the swap from the investment company with the fixed amount it would wish to receive on the notional principal at current market rates. Depending on the detailed terms of the swap agreement, it will be possible for the bank to adjust the floating rate payments to the investment company, i.e. to LIBOR plus or minus a number of basis points – minus in this example, to allow for the difference between the rates.

The receipts from the investment company can be discounted to a present value using the zero coupon rates. The figures here are for each 100 (nominal value) of bonds.

Year	Cash flow	Discount factor		Present value
1	7	$1/(1.08)$	$= 0.9259$	6.4815
2	7	$1/(1.0851)^2$	$= 0.8493$	5.9451
3	107	$1/(1.0877)^3$	$= 0.7771$	83.1489
		Total		95.5755

Therefore the net present value (NPV) is:

+ 95.5755   (value of swap receipts)
- 96.0000   (price of bond)
- 0.4245   i.e. 42.45 basis points

To bring the NPV to zero, i.e. to create a par swap, the swaps bank would pay a margin under LIBOR to the investment bank, on the floating side. The number of basis points is calculated by dividing the negative present value by the sum of the discount factors to arrive at an annuity.

$$\frac{-42.45 \text{ basis points}}{(0.9259 + 0.8493 + 0.7771)} = \frac{-42.45 \text{ bp}}{2.5523}$$

= - 16.6 basis points (negative, therefore the variable payments in the swap will be under LIBOR).

The swaps bank therefore will pay LIBOR minus 16.6 basis points in the swap, in return for an amount equal to the payments on the bond.

Conclusion

This introduction to the zero coupon swap curve does not go far into the technical details of setting rates for non-par swaps. However, the concept of the zero coupon (spot) rate is fundamental to swap market activities. If you develop your knowledge of swaps beyond this introductory level, you will have to know much more about how zero coupon rates are applied in practise.

Glossary

Arbitrage
Dealing in two or more markets at the same time or in similar products in the same market, to take advantage of temporary mis-pricing to make a profit.

Ask Rate
The price that a swaps bank would be willing to receive fixed-rate payments in a swap, against payment of a variable-rate benchmark, e.g. LIBOR.

Asset Swap
An interest rate or currency swap that changes the basis of income received on an investment. A coupon swap changes the basis of income received from fixed rate to floating rate or vice versa.

Assignment
The sale of a swap to a new third party, or buyout of a swap by a third party. The third party becomes a party to the swap.

Basis Point
One hundredth of 1% (0.01%).

Basis Swap
A swap from one floating rate to another, e.g. three-month LIBOR to six-month LIBOR, or six-month $ LIBOR to six-month euribor rate.

BBAIRS Terms
Standard terms for short-term interbank interest-rate swaps, provided by

the British Bankers' Association. Also used as the basis for setting terms for some swaps between banks and non-bank customers.

Bid Rate
The price at which a bank is willing to pay fixed-rate interest against receipt of variable rate (LIBOR) in an interest-rate swap.

Bond Basis
Swap rate based on the interest-rate convention for bonds. Dollar swap rates quoted on a bond basis assume a 365-day year for interest. Swaps arranged in association with a bond issue will have swap rates quoted on a bond basis.

Buyout
See Assignment.

Callable Swap
A swap that gives the fixed-rate payer an option to cancel the swap agreement, usually only on one specific future date.

Cocktail Swap
See Multi-legged Swap.

Counterparty
The other party to a contract or deal.

Coupon
The annual interest payable on a bond issue, expressed as a percentage of the nominal value of the bond.

Coupon Swap
An interest-rate swap in which the parties swap fixed for floating-rate payments. Also called a fixed/floating swap.

Cross-Currency Coupon Swap
A currency swap combined with an interest-rate coupon swap (a swap of

139

fixed-rate payments in one currency for floating-rate payments in another).

Currency Swap
A transaction in which two parties agree to swap fixed or floating-rate cash flows in different currencies for a specific period.

Eurobond
Marketable debt security issued outside the country in whose currency the debt is denominated.

Fixed Rate
An interest rate that does not vary during the life of a transaction.

Floating Rate
An interest rate that is reset at agreed intervals during the life of a transaction by reference to a benchmark rate of interest at a specific time on the reset date.

Generic Swap
A coupon swap that is traded for standard periods (two, three, four, five, seven years) and for round amounts of notional principal, and has a zero value when first transacted.

Hedge
Action or instrument for reducing or eliminating risk.

Index
General term for the benchmark interest rate used as the floating rate in a swap agreement, e.g. six-month sterling LIBOR.

ISDA
International Swaps and Derivatives Association that provides standardized documentation, conditions and procedures for swaps administration.

Liability Swap
A swap in which one party exchanges a stream of cash outflows for a

liability, e.g. a loan, into a different stream of outflows. For interest-rate swaps, a liability swap involves the exchange of a stream of payments at one interest rate for a stream of payments at another interest rate, over a term, typically of two to ten years.

LIBOR
London Interbank Offered Rate. Theoretically the rate at which two AAA-rated banks will lend to each other.

Market Maker
A bank, or a broker, willing to make two-way prices, i.e. a buying and selling rate, leaving the customer free to decide whether to deal at the bid or offer rate.

Matched Cash Flows
A situation where future receipts and payments are exactly equal and opposite. This term is used to refer to a swap arrangement in which a customer's payments on a loan are matched by swap receipts, or in which receipts from an investment are matched by swap payments.

Money-Market Basis
Swap rate based on the interest-rate convention for the money markets. Dollar swap payments on a money-market basis assume a 360-day year for interest.

Multi-Legged Swap
A number of swap agreements arranged by a bank in which the requirements of other counterparties to the swaps can be matched, leaving the bank with little or no interest rate or currency exposures of its own.

Notional Principal
The amount used to calculate interest payments in an interest-rate swap.

Offer
The price at which a bank is willing to receive fixed-rate interest against payment of a variable rate such as LIBOR.

Pab
An annual interest payment settled on a bond basis.

Pamm
Annual interest payments settled on a money-market basis.

Payer
The party in a swap transaction that pays a fixed rate and receives a floating rate.

Plain Vanilla Coupon Swap
See Generic Swap.

Present Value
A valuation in today's money of a stream of future cash flows, after allowing for interest costs. Present-value calculations are based on the premise that $1 in a future year is worth less than $1 now because less than $1 needs to be invested now to yield $1 in a future year the result of money's interest-earning capability over time. Cash flows in future years can be reduced to a present-value equivalent to assess investment yield potential or yield requirements.

Receiver
The party in a swap transaction that receives a fixed interest rate and pays a floating rate.

Reversal
Eliminating an existing swap by transacting a second swap in the opposite direction.

Sab
Semi-annual interest payments settled on a bond basis.

Samm
Semi-annual interest payments settled on a money-market basis.

Spread
The rate quoted on fixed-rate payments or receipts can be either an

absolute or a spread above the yield from an agreed fixed-rate instrument, such as Treasury bonds or UK gilts. The spread is the difference between the absolute price and the government bond yield.

Swap
An agreement between two parties to exchange a series of future payments. In an interest-rate swap, the exchange of payments is from one interest rate to another.

Swaps Market
Swaps activity by banks, brokers and corporations that exchange fixed and floating-rate payments with each other in various currencies. Transactions are arranged by telephone and fax.

Swap Rate
The interest rate in a swap agreement on which the regular exchange of cash flows during the term of the swap is based. Strictly speaking, a swap rate is not an interest rate because a swap involves the exchange of cash flows, not the exchange of loans or investments.

Swaption
Option to enter into a swap agreement.

Treasury Bond
Government debt, over 10 years in maturity at issue. Usually callable.

Treasury Yield
The yield to maturity on a Treasury bond or note that is nearest in maturity to a particular swap.

Index

Accounting for profits or losses on interest-rate swaps 121
Administration of swaps 104
Amortizing swaps 86
Anticipating interest-rate changes 31
Arbitrage 33
Arrangers 106
Arranging non-par value swaps 94
Arranging swaps 105
Asset swaps 3, 74
   features 77
   why use them 74
Assignment (buyout) 113

Banks as intermediaries 8
Banks as primary markets 105
Bank's role 44
Basis risk 121
Basis swaps 7
Bond basis 62
British Bankers' Association Interest Rate Swaps standard terms (BBAIRS) 110
Broking 44
Broking firms 107
Buyout 113

Changing the basis of interest payments 22
Closing out a swap 111
Combining coupon and basis swaps 30
Commodity swap 3
Contract terms 110
Coupon and basis swaps, combining 30
Coupon swaps 6
Credit arbitrage 33
Credit risk 48
   and swaps 116
Currency swap 2

Dates 16
Day-count conventions 63
Discount rate 95
Discount swaps 79

Equity swap 2
Event of default 110

FAS 115 122
Features of swaps 18

INDEX

Financial risk and swaps 116
Fixed payments valuation 95
Fixed rate
 payer 15
 receiver 15
Fixed-rate and floating-rate mix
 changing 27
Fixed-rate quotations 61
Floating-rate payments
 valuation 96
Floating-rate quotations 61
Forward curve analysis 132
Forward-start swaps 84

Generic swap 8, 95
Global risk management 44

Implied forward curve 133
Inability to borrow at a fixed
 rate 29
Interest payments, changing the
 basis of 22
Interest payments, reasons for
 changing basis of 26
Interest-rate changes,
 anticipating 31
Interest-rate swap 2
 accounting for profits or
  losses 121
 definition 6
 valuing 94
Intermediate banks 48
 and large swaps 49

International Swaps and
 Derivatives Association
 (ISDA) 110
ISDA documentation 110

Large swaps and intermediating
 bank 49
Liability swap 3
LIBOR 23
LIBOR-in-arrears swaps 87
Long-term borrowing 29

Market makers in swaps 106
Market-making in swaps 60
Master Swaps Agreement 111
Matched book dealers 106
Matched swap payments 66
Matching payment obligations 68
Matching requirements 45
Maturity risk 121
Measuring profitability 93
Money-market basis 62
Multi-legged swaps 46

Negotiating matched payments 66
Negotiating process 107
Netting of payments 13
Non-generic swaps 84
Non-par and par swaps 126
Non-par swaps valuation 98
Notional principal 10

147

Obtaining a zero coupon rate 127

Pa and sa 61
Pa bond basis 69
Par and non-par swaps 126
Payer and receiver 15
Payments 110
Payments under swap
  agreement 13
Plain vanilla coupon swap 84
Plain vanilla swap 8
Premium swaps 79
Price changes: market-making in
  swaps 60
Primary market: banks 105

Quantifying the credit risk 117

Rates received and paid 15
Reasons for swaps valuation 93
Receiver and payer 15
Regulation and financial risk 123
Reversal 113
Role of banks 44

Sa and pa 61
Sa bond basis 69
Samm basis 69
Small customers 47
Spread size 60
Swap
  features 18

negotiating process 109
payments 11
rates 15
spreads 57
terminology 109
timing 105
Swaps
  arranging 105
  administration 104
  and credit risk 116
  and financial risk 116
  and interest-rate risk 119
  and risk-taking 33
  bank and small customers 47
  bank as intermediary 9
  book 49
  prices screen 55
  rates 54
  rates: pay rates and receive
    rates 54
  reasons for valuation 93
  users 104

Tax positions 49
Term of a swap 17
Termination 110, 111
Terminology 109
Types of swap 2

Up-front compensation
  payment 79
Uses of liability swaps 22

Valuation of fixed payments 95
Valuation of floating-rate
  payments 96
Valuation of non-par swaps 98
Valuation of swaps 92
Valuing an interest-rate swap 94

Warehousing 44

Zero coupon rate 126
  and non-par swaps 133
  obtaining 127
Zero coupon swap curve 131
Zero coupon swap rates 95

Notes

Notes